SIMPLY **REDWORK**

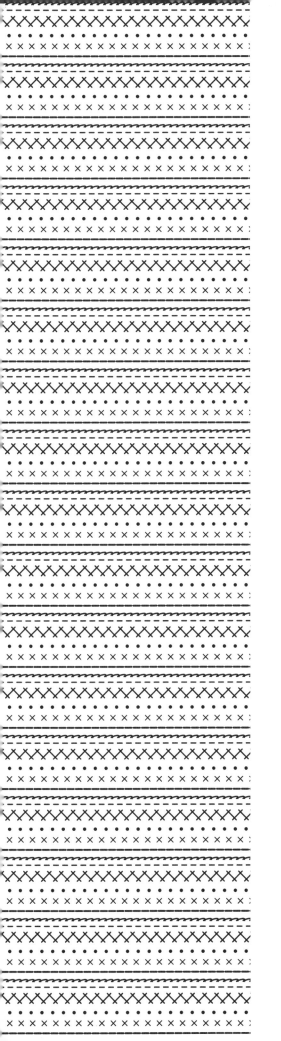

SIMPLY
REDWORK

Mandy Shaw

D&C
David and Charles

www.stitchcraftcreate.co.uk

Contents

The Author

Mandy Shaw describes herself as a maker of all things lovely, and she loves to share her inspirations with you. This will be her fifth book for David & Charles, and her ideas are still flowing. She lives in East Sussex in her homemade home with her large family and continues to teach and travel around the UK to share her passion for sewing crafts. She has appeared on Kirstie Allsopp's TV shows and contributed to two of Kirstie's books.

Mandy is a guest presenter on Create and Craft TV and frequently contributes to craft and patchwork magazines across the globe.

Introduction

Why redwork? Well, it's simple – the colour is chosen for you, the stitches are easy and the results are just lovely, so I think you'll agree, why not redwork?

I am drawn to the colour red, especially a good dark blood red. When I visit fabric shops I stroke the red fabrics first! Red is the colour of passion, energy and love. In China it represents good luck, happiness and prosperity; in India it symbolizes purity and is often used for wedding gowns. All the projects in this book reflect my love and passion for sewing, so red is the perfect choice.

Red had always been a difficult dye to make so when in the late 19th century a technique was found to produce a colourfast, non-fading cotton thread, embroidering in red and making red-and-white quilts became very popular, and redwork as we know it was born. It was such a simple idea: outline a drawing in a basic stitch in one colour – no elaborate tools required, just a needle, thread and scissors. It was easy for everyone to do and the results simply beautiful. I have created this collection of projects to share my passion for redwork with you, using my own drawings and doodles. So get ready to roll out the red carpet and shine!

This book is dedicated to all my customers and students who want to make my designs: without your support there would be no point.

History of Redwork

I was just so delighted to find this vintage 1920s penny square quilt on an antique stand at a quilt show. It was just a top and it stayed that way for years; although it was always my intention to hand quilt it, eventually I had it long-arm quilted to preserve it. This made it much more stable so that I could use it in my lectures and display it on my hall wall, where it has been so admired that it inspired me to make my own version. It was from this that my redwork hearts were born. My vintage quilt is from the United States, where redwork has been so popular since the late 19th century. Researching the history of the quilt's motifs, I was delighted to find that the story of redwork began much closer to home.

In 1872, the School of Art Needlework was founded by Victoria Welby, who received help from William Morris, his daughter May and his friends in the Arts and Crafts Movement. The word 'Royal' was added in 1875 when Queen Victoria consented to become its first patron. Originally housed above a bonnet shop in Kensington, London, the Royal School of Needlework (the 'Art' was dropped in the 1920s) moved to its current home at Hampton Court Palace in 1987. Today, the RSN is famous the world over as an international centre for the art of hand embroidery.

In 1876, the year after it gained royal patronage, the Royal School of Art Needlework, along with over 14,000 other businesses and organizations, exhibited at the Philadelphia Centennial Exhibition, the first official World's Fair. As well as an opportunity to explore the world's cultures, the exposition was a springboard for new inventions and scientific advancements. Alexander Graham Bell's telephone and Heinz ketchup made their first appearance here, along with the British penny-farthing and the right arm of the Statue of Liberty (the revenue collected to climb the ladder to the viewing balcony was used to help fund the rest of the statue!).

The Royal School of Art Needlework showcased its work with a simple hand surface embroidery sewn with a backstitch, then known as the Kensington stitch after the school's location. The Americans loved the new technique and they began to embroider designs with simple outlines to decorate household furnishings and wares.

At around the same time, synthetic dyes became readily available in a variety of colours although these cheaper red threads faded to a rose or brownish red. Turkey red, even though more expensive, was valued for its durability and the fact that it would not bleed or run or fade. (Turkey red is a dye process producing a rich, colourfast cloth, brought to Europe by Jewish and Syrian dyers, 'Turkey' being the catchall name used for the Middle East.) The process of using this dye was long and complicated and even to this day red dye is expensive to produce.

The advances in these red threads and the inspiration provided by the Royal School of Art Needlework led to the explosion of simple outline designs on a white background, embroidered in red, now known as redwork. Pre-printed squares were later sold with all sorts of images from birds and flowers, to nursery rhyme characters and US presidents. Used to decorate items for the home, these were often made into quilts just like my vintage quilt. With the resurgence of craft and quilting in the last few years, redwork has made a comeback and its simple stitchery is once again very popular.

Get Ready to Stitch

If you are new to stitching, this chapter will give you all the advice you need to begin with confidence. Luckily most items required for stitching can be found in an everyday sewing basket. The embroideries are hand-stitched, but a sewing machine has been used to make up most of the projects, and I have included some best practice tips here.

I have given details of the fabrics and threads I have used with tips to help you get started with your own sewing stash. There is a guide to the different ways you can transfer embroidery motifs to your fabric, and the section on working the stitches has instructions for both right- and left-handed stitchers. So what are you waiting for? Get stitching!

Fabrics, Threads and Tools

Just so long as it's natural and a needle slices through it like butter, I will stitch it. I have an ever-growing collection of fabrics and threads, and I encourage you to start your fabric stash today. Look out for lovely linens and cottons wherever you go.

LINENS AND COTTONS

Embroider a small test piece to see if you like the way your chosen fabric stitches before you embark on a large project. Traditionally, an evenweave cotton was used for redwork embroidery, but I have stitched on 100 per cent fine cottons, linens and calicos. My favourite is a linen/cotton mix, which I think gives you the best of both worlds – a rustic evenweave with a soft touch.

I love to scour second-hand shops looking for opportunities to recycle clothing and household linens to build my fabric collection. I rummage for recycled tray cloths and linens whenever the opportunity arises!

FELT

There is really only one felt that I would recommend you use and that is wool felt. Without the wool, felt will not last and is poor quality. At the very least, you should choose a wool/rayon mix felt.

TIP

Fabrics are often treated with a dressing so that they look good for selling; if this is the case, I advise that you gently wash the fabric before stitching as it will be easier to work with.

Fabrics, Threads and Tools

THREADS

Although I have used coton à broder for most of the project embroideries, I heartily encourage you to explore stitching with other types of thread. The threads I prefer are described below but do experiment with other thicknesses and types.

Coton à broder A favourite of mine, this single strand thread has a matt finish. It is available in different widths in several colours, so if you wish you can explore bluework, purplework or whatever your favourite colour thread might be! I prefer no. 16 which is quite thick and ideal for redwork, blanket stitching, outlining, backstitching and quilting. While I have stitched the project embroideries with DMC threads you can, of course, use other brands, such as Anchor for example, if you prefer.

Perle This high-sheen single strand thread has a slight twist to it. It is available in skeins or balls in different thicknesses from no. 3 (thick) to no. 12 (thin), and the one I prefer is no. 8. It produces a thick stitching line with a slight texture to it and it makes a good substitute for coton à broder, but use it on strong simple lines only.

Stranded cotton (floss) This is available in a skein consisting of six strands, which can be pulled out individually for use. It is most usual to use two strands in the needle, but for fine detail you can use just one strand, and for a chunkier stitching line use three or more. This gives you the adaptability of being able to sew thicker and thinner in the same colour should you choose to.

Cosmo multi work 322 A range of embroidery threads (by Lecien) that come off the spool in two strands, ready to stitch, and they are the perfect weight for redwork. There is a lovely pinky red shade in the range.

Maderia Lana I used this machine embroidery thread for the stitched panel of the project bag (see Extra Inspirations). This thread is finer than coton à broder so it was great for this more detailed design. The wool content of the Maderia Lana produces a slightly fluffy effect rather than the flat sheen achieved with traditional threads. (By the way, Aurifil produce a Lana wool thread in a good red, shade 8260, and this is finer still.)

TIP

I keep my DMC threads wound onto my flat card thread spools. I have provided the thread spool template (see Templates and Motifs) for you to make some of your own. Trace the shape off onto a medium-weight card and cut out. Wind your thread onto the spool and tuck in the end. Don't forget to make a note of the thread colour/thickness in the heart at the top of the spool!

THREAD-WISE

- You can substitute two strands of stranded cotton (floss) or a single perle thread for a single coton à broder thread.

- Good-quality thread brands will be colourfast; they will not run and spoil your work. If using recycled threads of an unknown origin, always test for colourfastness before using.

- Be aware threads can deteriorate with age – colours fade and they may be weakened.

- As well as embroidery threads, you will also need sewing threads for project make up. Use a good-quality thread to match your fabric.

TIP

Here's a useful tip to keep Anchor threads neat and ready to use: remove the paper label and unwind the skein. Cut through all the threads at the knot. Fold in half and place the loop end over a small door knob. Divide into three and plait firmly to the end. Pull a new thread from the looped end. The remaining threads will stay plaited – the thread removed is the perfect length for sewing.

NEEDLES

I have, at last, after many years of experimenting, found my favourite needle: a chenille number 24. It is short but has a wide eye for easy threading of thicker threads. It is also very sharp, piercing the fabric easily and allowing the thread to be pulled through with very little friction.

Threading a needle To use a needle threader, push the wire loop through the needle eye; push the thread through the wire loop. Gently pull the needle threader back out of the hole and it will bring the thread with it.

TIP

I am a keen recycler of fabrics, but I'd urge caution with needles and threads – old needles may develop little rust spots, and thread deteriorates over time and you can never be sure that it will be colourfast.

OTHER ESSENTIALS

The beauty of redwork is that you need very little, if any, specialized equipment. Your essential kit comprises a small pair of embroidery scissors for cutting threads, a needle case to store your needles in, and a bag to keep your work clean and safe. In addition, I always make sure I have the following:

Iron-on lightweight interfacing I always fuse lightweight interfacing to the back of my embroidery work, as it means I can skip across from one motif to another and the threads will not show from the front. Fuse the interfacing to the wrong side of the fabric using an iron set to a medium heat: beware as a hot iron will melt the interfacing.

Wadding (batting) I sometimes back my embroidery work with wadding (batting) so the stitches create a quilted effect.

Spray adhesive When I use wadding (batting), I more often than not use spray adhesive to fix it in position. It is much quicker than tacking (basting), and there is the added advantage that you can peel it off and reposition it if you need to. However, it is important to remember that you should only ever spray the wadding (batting) and never the embroidered work to avoid marking the fabric.

Transferring the Motifs

Before beginning your embroidery you need to transfer your chosen design onto your fabric. There are many ways to do this. Choose the method you prefer, and remember you must be able to see the outline clearly to embroider it, but it should not be visible on the finished project.

PENS

Fade away pens Beware as marks made with these may fade before you have finished stitching. Do not iron the marked lines or expose them to heat as they may become permanent or leave an unsightly stain.

Washable pens Lines marked with these pens will wash out or they can be erased with a damp cotton bud if you prefer, but test on your fabric first. I once had a nasty experience where years later a yellow stain could be seen on my embroidery where the marked line had been.

Permanent pen It is very important for you to be able to see the marked lines clearly. This pen's fine tip makes a clear, strong line, especially on smaller projects. The line it makes is, however, very permanent.

DRESSMAKER'S CARBON PAPER

This is available in white, blue, pink and yellow. Place the paper on the fabric, right sides together. Place the tracing or template on top and draw around the design with a ball point pen. Work on a hard, flat surface and press very firmly (it may be a good idea to tape down the fabric so that it doesn't move). The transferred line can sometimes be quite thick and it doesn't always come out successfully.

LIGHT BOX

A great aid for tracing motifs onto lighter fabrics, a light box is both reasonably priced and readily available; alternatively, you can make one from a strong plastic or heavy cardboard box. Fix a light fitting inside and clip a piece of perspex on top.

IRON-ON TRANSFER PENCIL

Use to trace the motif onto tracing paper. Place the tracing paper onto your fabric, right sides facing and iron (without steam). This transferral method is useful for fabrics that you cannot see through, such as thicker linens and wools, but the motif will be reversed. The transferred line is permanent and cannot be erased so you will need to hide it with your embroidery stitches, and you must sharpen the pencil frequently to avoid a thick drawn line.

PENCIL

This is my preferred method for tracing a design when I can see through the fabric. If you use either pencils sharpened to a point or good quality propelling pencils, the mark will be so fine that it will not require erasing.

WATERCOLOUR PENCIL

This is another great option but be sure to keep the leads well sharpened to maintain a fine line. The marks will wash out when rubbed with a damp cotton bud.

DRESSMAKER'S PENCIL

These are readily available in most fabric shops, and come in pink, blue and white for marking both light and dark fabrics. It is not possible to get a fine point on the pencil, but as the marked line can be brushed off or washed out, this is not such a problem.

TIP

As an alternative to a light box, tape the design to the window, then tape your fabric on top and trace off.

Project-Making Techniques

I have designed 15 projects for you to embellish with redwork embroidery, including two eye-catching quilts, which are perfect for showcasing the redwork hearts that I have designed. All the instruction you require to make the projects is provided in clear, concise step-by-step detail, with useful illustrations to help explain the trickier techniques.

SEWING BY HAND OR MACHINE

I have used a sewing machine to make all of the projects in this book, although they can be made entirely by hand if you so choose. But if you have access to a sewing machine, do use it. It is so much faster, leaving more time for the stitching, which is the fun bit. Some helpful tips on using a sewing machine are included here. Whether you choose to stitch your chosen projects by hand or machine, there are a couple of hand finishing stitches you will need – ladder stitch and slip stitch.

USING A SEWING MACHINE

A sewing machine will produce much stronger seams and a more uniform, professional result than hand stitching when making up the projects. It is well worth taking a little time to get to know your sewing machine better. The best way to do this is to read the instruction manual that came with it, and to test stitch on the fabrics you have selected for your project.

The commonest problems you are likely to encounter are poor tension and missing stitches, and these are usually easy to solve.

Poor tension If the stitching on the back and the front of the fabric is not perfectly balanced, check that you have threaded the machine correctly and that the bobbin you are using is the right one (there are commonly two sizes) and that it has been inserted the correct way.

Missing stitches When was the last time you changed the needle? A needle needs to be changed after every major project. Always use a good-quality needle, size 80 (12) or 90 (14).

To get the best from your machine, keep it well maintained. Use the special brushes provided to clean away the dust and fabric residue that builds up after each project, paying particular attention to the bobbin and its casing. If the manual advises it, give your machine a light oil. Make sure you use oil that is specifically designed for sewing machines. If these general maintenance tips do not solve the problems you are experiencing, seek the advice of your local service engineer.

TIP

As long as you sew slowly and pin your fabric correctly, there is no reason why you cannot machine stitch over pins.

LADDER STITCH

This is used to close a seam on a stuffed item or for sewing two folded edges together. The stitches look like a ladder until pulled tight to close the seam. Knot the end of the thread and start from inside the opening to hide the knot. Take straight stitches into the folded fabric, stitching into each edge in turn. After a few stitches pull the thread taut to draw up the stitches and close the gap.

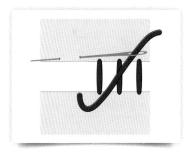

SLIP STITCH

This stitch is also used to close gaps in seams. When worked neatly, it is almost invisible. Work from right to left, picking up a tiny piece of the fabric from one seam edge. Insert the needle into the other seam fold and move the needle along 3mm (⅛in). Push the needle out into the seam edge and repeat.

Working the Stitches

As redwork is all about simple line drawings worked in one colour thread, the stitches you use should be simple too. The motifs are worked with simple outline stitches, such as backstitch and stem stitch, which are very quick to learn, and because of their simplicity you can easily achieve a nice even stitch. Once you have mastered these stitches, it will be very obvious to you which is your favourite – mine has always been the backstitch but I sewed a project for the book in stem stitch and loved the result, so have a play and see which you prefer. In addition to the outlining stitches, a few other stitches are occasionally used for a little embellishment and highlighting of the designs, from a smattering of French knots to a sprinkling of cross stitches, plus a few more besides.

STARTING AND FINISHING STITCHING

- Iron-on lightweight interfacing can be ironed onto the back of the fabric prior to working the embroidery to hide knots and stray ends.

- Thread your needle – never use more than a short arm's length of thread at one time as it will be more prone to knotting, and more vulnerable to fraying and splitting.

- Start the embroideries with a small knot on the wrong side of the work. To avoid the knot being seen from the front of the work, do keep it small.

- When rejoining a thread, use your needle to weave the new thread into the previous stitches.

- When you have finished your embroidery, weave the thread into the previous sewn work.

- Do not leave long strands hanging on the back as these may show through on the front.

- Keep your embroidery and fabric scissors sharp and never be tempted to use them for cutting paper.

USING AN EMBROIDERY HOOP

It is a matter of personal preference as to whether or not you use an embroidery hoop to keep your fabric taut while stitching. I prefer not to as I find it gets in my way and yet I still produce lovely work with no lumps or bumps. Embroidery hoops come in two parts, a smaller hoop and a slightly larger one with a tension screw on one side. They can be made of wood or plastic, although plastic ones may not have a tension screw. Place the fabric you are going to embroider over the smaller hoop. Place the larger hoop over the fabric and push it onto the smaller hoop – you will find the larger hoop is stretchy enough to enable you to do this. Pull the fabric taut and tighten the tension screw. The fabric is now ready to embroider.

TIP

The stitches required for each project are listed beneath the 'you will need' listing. Practise them first on a linen scrap following the instructions for right- or left-handed stitchers as appropriate.

Backstitch

This is the perfect stitch when a well-defined fine outline is required. It sews around corners and awkward shapes easily, and it looks good worked in all types of thread.

Right-handers. Work from right to left. Begin by bringing the needle up a little ahead of where you want the line of stitching to start. Take the needle to the right, to the start position, back through the fabric to make a stitch, and bring it out to the left past the first stitch (Fig. 1R). Each time a stitch is made, the thread passes back to fill the gap, for small stitches of an equal length (Fig. 2R).

Left-handers. Work from left to right. Begin by bringing the needle up a little ahead of where you want to start the stitching. Take the needle to the left, to the start position, back through the fabric to make a stitch, and bring it out to the right past the first stitch (Fig. 1L). Each time a stitch is made, the thread passes back to fill the gap, for small stitches of an equal length (Fig. 2L).

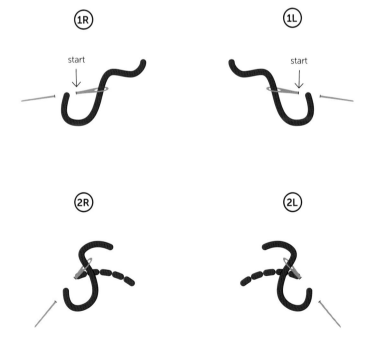

TIP

To create a nice even flow in the design, do be sure to stitch directly in the previous hole that you made as little gaps can be unsightly.

Stem Stitch

An outline stitch with neatly overlapping lines. It sews around gentle curves but not tight shapes and points, so it is best used for very simple shapes that are continuous. As this stitch almost doubles up on itself, it is best not to use the thicker threads.

Right-handers. Work from left to right. Bring the needle up at the start point and make a stitch forward. Take a tiny stitch backwards from right to left. Pull the needle through, keeping the thread above the needle (Fig. 1R). Take another small stitch to the right bringing the needle out near the hole of the last stitch (Fig. 2R). As you continue to stitch the stitches take on a diagonal slant (Fig. 3R).

Left-handers. Work from right to left. Bring the needle up at the start point and make a stitch backward. Take a tiny stitch forwards from left to right. Pull the needle through, keeping the thread above the needle (Fig. 1L). Take another small stitch to the left bringing the needle out near the hole of the last stitch (Fig. 2L). As you continue to stitch the stitches take on a diagonal slant (Fig. 3L).

TIP

Keep your stitches quite small as they do tend to grow in length.

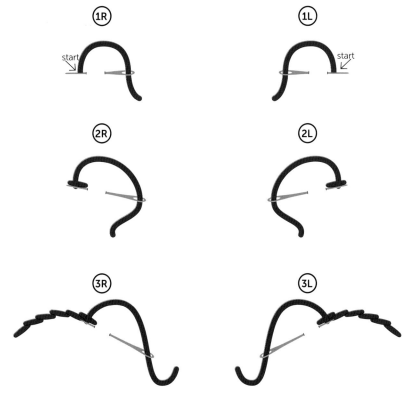

Running Stitch

Run the needle in and out of the fabric for a simple but versatile line stitch. The most basic of all stitches, I do not use this to outline the redwork motifs, but as an accent to create a flow or highlight within a shape.

Right-handers. Work from right to left. Bring the needle up through the fabric, make a stitch, and bring the needle down through the fabric. Repeat, making sure the stitches and the spaces between them are the same size (Fig. 1R).

Left-handers. Work from left to right. Bring the needle up through the fabric, make a stitch, and bring the needle down through the fabric. Repeat, making sure the stitches and the spaces between them are the same size (Fig. 1L).

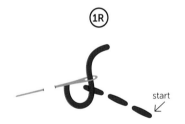

TIP

You can take more than one stitch on your needle at a time, but take care to keep stitches even.

Herringbone Stitch

This stitch needs a little practise to master it but once you have, it's very decorative. I have used it to aid the quilting of the redwork hearts quilt, working it around the embroidered blocks. It does not sew around curves very well so it is best worked in straight lines.

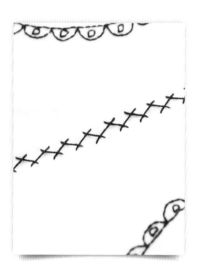

Right-handers. Work from left to right. Bring the needle up below the line of your chosen motif, cross over to the top right and take a little stitch to the left above the line (Fig. 1R). Cross over to the bottom right, and take a little stitch to the left. The needle should come out directly below the stitch above. Continue to line up the top end of a diagonal stitch with the bottom start of another for a nice, even line of stitching (Fig. 2R).

Left-handers. Work from right to left. Bring the needle up below the line of your chosen motif, cross over to the top left and take a little stitch to the right above the line (Fig. 1L). Cross over to the bottom left, and take a little stitch to the right. The needle should come out directly below the stitch above. Continue to line up the top end of a diagonal stitch with the bottom start of another for a nice, even line of stitching (Fig. 2L).

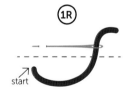

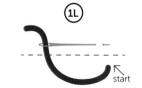

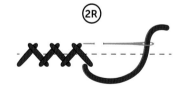

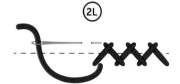

TIP

I love the look of this stitch, but you should take care that your stitches do not get bigger as you go along, as mine often do. It is worth persisting, as the results can look fantastic. The seam lines run through the middle of the stitch.

Blanket Stitch

I have used this stitch to create interest or to highlight a shape, but it would be far too busy to use as an outline stitch for your redwork motifs! It's my favourite stitch to appliqué a shape into place.

Right-handers. Work from left to right. Bring the needle up on the line of the motif or at the edge of the appliqué. Take a stitch down from your start point and bring the needle back where you started keeping the thread to the left (Fig. 1R). Insert the needle to the right of the first stitch, down from the line or edge, and bring it back out on the line or edge, making sure the thread is behind the needle. Pull through (Fig.2R). Continue repeating to make a line of stitches.

Left-handers. Work from right to left. Bring the needle up on the line of the motif or at the edge of the appliqué. Take a stitch down from your start point and bring the needle back where you started keeping the thread to the right (Fig. 1L). Insert the needle to the left of the first stitch, down from the line or edge, and bring it back out on the line or edge, making sure the thread is behind the needle. Pull through (Fig. 2L). Continue repeating to make a line of stitches.

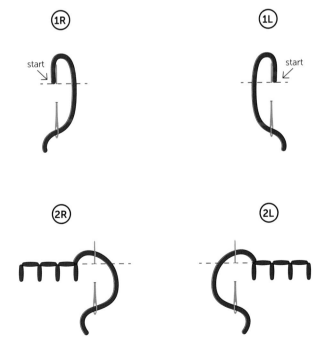

TIP

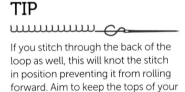

If you stitch through the back of the loop as well, this will knot the stitch in position preventing it from rolling forward. Aim to keep the tops of your stitches level.

French Knot

Strictly the stitch shown is known as a colonial knot, which is much easier to work than the traditional French knot, and it creates a nice tight little bud. I use this stitch mainly for eyes, flower centres and decorative details.

Right-handers. Bring the needle up from the back of the fabric, and wrap the thread around the needle two or three times. Put the needle back into the fabric close to where it originally came out. Do not go back into the same hole otherwise the knot will be lost (Fig. 1R). Before pulling the needle back through the fabric, gently pull up the thread that is twisted around the needle. Place your fingernail over the twist and pull through (Fig. 2R).

Left-handers. Bring the needle up from the back of the fabric, and wrap the thread around the needle two or three times. Put the needle back into the fabric close to where it originally came out. Do not go back into the same hole otherwise the knot will be lost (Fig. 1L). Before pulling the needle back through the fabric, gently pull up the thread that is twisted around the needle. Place your fingernail over the twist and pull through (Fig. 2L).

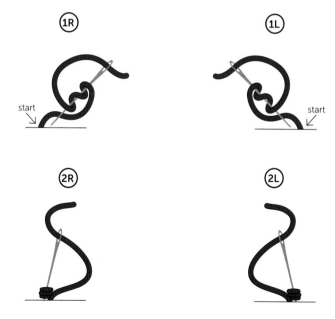

TIP

For a larger or smaller knot, wrap the thread around the needle more or fewer times.

Cross Stitch

Discover the decorative power of the individual cross stitch. To create a star stitch, work one cross stitch on top of the other.

Right-handers. Work from left to right. Bring the needle up through the fabric. Take a stitch diagonally from the top left to the bottom right and bring the needle back out at the lower left corner (Fig. 1R). Take a stitch diagonally to the top right corner and bring the needle back out where the next cross stitch is required. Pull the needle through to complete the cross stitch (Fig. 2R).

Left-handers. Work from right to left. Bring the needle up through the fabric. Take a stitch diagonally from the top right to the bottom left and bring the needle back out at the lower right corner (Fig. 1L). Take a stitch diagonally to the top left corner and bring the needle back out where the next cross stitch is required. Pull the needle through to complete the cross stitch (Fig. 2L).

TIP

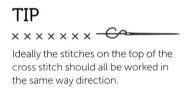

Ideally the stitches on the top of the cross stitch should all be worked in the same way direction.

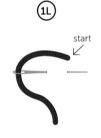

Motifs and
Projects

This is an exciting chapter where I have designed one or more projects for you to sew using the theme of each of the stitch motif hearts displayed on my redwork quilts.

Some of the projects are very practical, such as the sewing purse and the key tidy, while others are perfect to decorate the home or to give as gifts, such as the heart cushion, the hanging heart and the flying dove. Some will be loved by the family, such as the whimsical polar bear cake band and the little hands place mat, while others are just for you, the daisy brooch, the scissors keeper and the alphabet tags, for example.

All of these designs can be personalized by you by using the additional motifs that I have supplied in Templates and Motifs.

Stitch Motif:
Heart

The heart shape is one of the most recognized symbols on earth and it goes back a very long way – there are even prehistoric cave paintings of hearts, although the meaning of the symbol in this context is unknown. It is thought that the shape we know today may be derived from leaves, especially those of the ivy, which symbolize longevity and endurance. The ivy leaf/heart symbol can be found on the decorative art of the Minoans, the Ancient Egyptians, the Ancient Romans and the Ancient Greeks, who associated ivy with Dionysus, the god of wine, passion and all things sensual, so perhaps this is where the romantic connection was first made. I have designed a wonderful cushion to celebrate this universal symbol for love.

For how to embroider the Heart heart design see Redwork Quilts: Embroidering the Heart Designs.

HEART PROJECT:
Heart Cushion

The design for this cushion has been influenced by European folk art and embroidery, and I have also been inspired by the work of paper cutting artists, such as Rob Ryan, who make amazing pictures out of cutwork paper. I have worked the embroidery onto white linen fabric, but calico fabric would work just as well. The embroidery panel has been made up into an envelope-back cushion cover. Cushions are a great way of displaying your work and they make wonderful house-warming gifts, but this design would also look great as a framed picture.

Heart Cushion

YOU WILL NEED

21.5 x 21.5cm (8$\frac{1}{2}$ x 8$\frac{1}{2}$in) white linen fabric for front panel

30cm (12in) of 107cm (42in) wide red dot fabric for borders and backing

One skein of DMC 815 coton à broder no. 16

32 x 32cm (12$\frac{1}{2}$ x 12$\frac{1}{2}$in) cotton/polyester mix wadding (batting)

130cm (50in) of wide red ric-rac

30 x 30cm (12 x 12in) feather pillow

FINISHED SIZE

30 x 30cm (12 x 12in)

STITCHES USED

Backstitch

French knot

Cross stitch

TO MAKE THE HEART CUSHION

1. From the red dot fabric, cut the following pieces:

Two 6.5 x 21.5cm (2$\frac{1}{2}$ x 8$\frac{1}{2}$in) strips for the top and bottom borders

Two 32 x 6.5cm (12$\frac{1}{2}$ x 2$\frac{1}{2}$in) strips for the side borders

Two 32 x 21.5cm (12$\frac{1}{2}$ x 8$\frac{1}{2}$in) pieces for the backing panels.

2. Transfer the heart cushion design (see Templates and Motifs) onto the 21.5cm (8$\frac{1}{2}$in) linen square using your preferred method (see Transferring the Designs).

3. Pin, then sew the top and bottom red dot border strips to the linen square, using a 6mm (¼in) seam. Then pin and sew the two longer red dot strips to each side to complete the preparation of the front panel. Press well.

4. Take your piece of wadding (batting) and lightly spray with spray adhesive, while closely following the manufacturer's instructions. Smooth the prepared front panel on top of the wadding (batting) and secure in place by stitching 6mm (¼in) all the way around the outside of the linen square.

5. Embroider the heart design using backstitch, working French knots in the centre of the hearts and for birds' eyes, and a single cross stitch in the oval beneath the centre top heart. Sew a quilting stitch border 6mm (¼in) in from the edge of the linen square (this is like a long running stitch).

6. Check your cushion top measures 32 x 32cm (12½ x 12½in) and trim if necessary. Take the ric-rac and, starting halfway down one side of the right side of the cushion top, pin on the braid all the way around, aligning the edge of the ric-rac with the raw edge of the fabric and gently curving the braid around the corners. Tack (baste) the ric-rac in place 6mm (¼in) from the edge, sewing down the middle of the braid, so that when the cushion is turned right side out, only little half moons will show.

7. To make the envelope-back, take the remaining two red dot fabric rectangles and turn under 6mm (¼in) along one long edge of each, turn

under again and stitch the hem in place. Overlap the hemmed edges (right sides facing up), so that the two rectangles measure 32 x 32cm (12½ x 12½in) and pin in place.

8. Pin the envelope-back to the cushion front, right sides together, and sew around the outside edge, sewing on the same line as the ric-rac. Snip the corners and trim the seams. Zigzag over the seam to prevent fraying and turn the cushion cover right way out.

Fill the finished cover with the pillow and take a seat!

TIP

Ric-rac frays badly, so when you start and end your stitching, fold back the ric-rac end so that the raw edges are in the seam allowance. This may mean that the humps do not perfectly align at these points, but this is preferable to frayed ends. Remember to ease the braid around the corner; if you go into the square corners it will create ugly points.

Stitch Motif:
Polar Bear

The polar bear is a beautiful and magnificent beast. Its Latin name, *Ursus maritimus*, means sea bear, and it is, indeed, an excellent swimmer. The polar bear's skin is actually black but its hollow hairs reflect the light to make it appear white. When first born, a polar bear cub is the weight of an adult guinea pig, yet it will grow up to become the largest carnivore on the planet. Roaming the Arctic Circle in search of seals, polar bears have no natural predator, yet they are a threatened species because of climate change. My polar bear wrist support will help you to remember to do your little bit to help save our planet and these incredible creatures, and make disposable party decorations a thing of the past with my easy-to-make adjustable cake band.

For how to embroider the Polar Bear heart design see Redwork Quilts: Embroidering the Heart Designs.

POLAR BEAR PROJECT:
Wrist Support

I first made this little bear as a small soft toy before realizing it was the perfect size for a wrist support when using a computer mouse. I then went on to play with this pattern further, enlarging it and using different fabrics, and so the polar bear has grown since to became a neck support for my grandson when he is sitting in his car seat – what next?

Wrist Support

YOU WILL NEED

25 x 20cm (10 x 8in) white wool felt

Small piece of red felt

One skein of DMC 815 coton à broder no. 16

Handful of polyester toy filling

Plastic pellets (optional)

FINISHED SIZE

15 x 11cm (5³/₄ x 4¹/₄in)

STITCHES USED

Blanket stitch

Backstitch

French knot

TO MAKE THE WRIST SUPPORT

1. Trace the polar bear body and the polar bear head (see Templates and Motifs) and cut out to give you your pattern pieces.

2. Fold your piece of white felt in half and pin the pattern pieces onto it. Cut around the pattern pieces to give you two body pieces and two head pieces. Mark the polar bear's facial features onto one of the head pieces using a fine pencil or fade-away pen.

3. Using the small heart motif marked on the polar bear's body pattern, cut out a heart from the scrap of red felt and stitch it onto the bear's rump as shown on the pattern

4. Pin the two body pieces together and hand sew around the edge using coton à broder and blanket stitch, leaving a small gap for stuffing. Gently stuff the body with your toy filling,

paying particular attention to the legs and arms. Continue the blanket stitch to sew the opening closed.

5. Stitch and stuff the head in the same way as the body, then embroider the lower facial features using backstitch, working the nose with five long straight stitches worked in a triangle shape from the top of the nose to a single point at the base of the nose. Define the ear shape with backstitch and work French knots for the eyes and single stitches for the eyebrows.

6. Placing the head at the narrower (arms) end of the body, sew or glue it in on at a jaunty angle, to help to create character.

Pop your polar bear on your desk and get typing.

TIP

To achieve a nice shape, stuff the polar bear with little pea-size balls of toy filling. Alternatively, fill it with plastic pellets to give weight.

TIP

When working the French knots for the eyes, take the thread through to the back of the head to make an indentation, as this helps to create a bit of character.

POLAR BEAR PROJECT:
Cake Band

Baking and sewing are all the rage at the moment, so why not combine the two with this oh-so-clever, easy-to-adjust cake band. It is 6cm (2½in) high but the width is easy to alter. Mine was made to fit a cake with a circumference of 60cm (24in). If you want to adapt the cake band to a larger cake size, cut your fabric and wadding (batting) strips to measure the circumference of your cake tin plus 5cm (2in) for an overlap. The cake band is washable so it can be used time and time again.

Cake Band

YOU WILL NEED

6.5 x 65cm (2½ x 26in) white cotton main fabric

6.5 x 65cm (2½ x 26in) backing fabric

6.5 x 65cm (2½ x 26in) thin wadding (batting)

One skein of DMC 815 coton à broder no. 16

143cm (56in) of 18mm (1¹/₁₆in) ready-made bias binding with lace edge

FINISHED SIZE

6.5 x 65cm (2½ x 26in)

STITCHES USED

Backstitch

French knot

TO MAKE THE CAKE BAND

1. Transfer the polar bear motifs, or motifs of your choosing (see Templates and Motifs), onto the white cotton fabric strip using your preferred method (see Transferring the Designs). I chose to repeat the polar bear motifs in groups of three, with a front-facing bear being flanked by right-facing and left-facing bears to either side.

2. Take your piece of wadding (batting) and lightly spray it on one side with spray adhesive following the manufacturer's instructions, then smooth it onto the back (unmarked side) of the white cotton fabric strip.

3. Embroider your design with the coton à broder. The snowballs and polar bears were stitched with backstitch and the polar bears' eyes were worked with French knots; their freckles were worked with very small single stitches and their claws with slightly longer single stitches.

4. Once your embroidery is complete, lightly spray the back of the wadding (batting) with spray adhesive and smooth the backing fabric onto it, trimming if necessary.

5. Starting at one end of the cake band, open out the binding and place the cake band in between the fold; pin and tack (baste) in place. Machine stitch all the way along the edge to the end of the cake band (Fig. 1). Raising the needle, take the cake band away from the sewing machine, and open out the binding flat along the next edge so that the cake band is butting up against the fold and there is a 45 degree angle fold on the binding at the corner edge. Fold the binding back in along the edge to mitre the corner beautifully (see Fig. 2). Lower the needle and continue to stitch along the next edge. Mitre each corner in the same way. When you reach your starting point, tuck under the raw edge of the binding to neaten before completing your stitching.

6. The cake band is secured in place with pins, which allows it to be adjusted to fit different-sized cakes. I recommend you use three pins with knobs on the end, so that they are decorative as well as being easy to see to remove.

Wrap the finished cake band around your cake and get ready to blow out the candles.

TIP

Use the additional motifs provided in the Templates and Motifs section to design a cake band to suit the occasion, or use the alphabet to personalize it by embroidering a name or simply the event being celebrated.

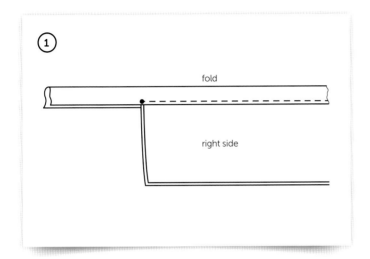

① fold

right side

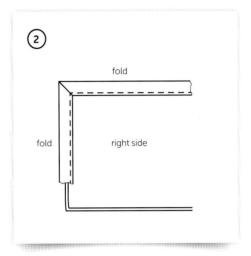

② fold

fold

right side

Stitch Motif:
Scissors

'We are but two halves of a pair of scissors, when apart...
but together we are something.' Charles Dickens, *Martin Chuzzlewit*

Once upon a time the city of Sheffield, Great Britain, had 150 small scissor-making companies. Sadly, now there are only a couple left. One of these companies, Ernest Wright & Sons, has just taken on a new young apprenctice to help preserve the future of scissor making in Great Britain. Treat yourself to a pair of scissors that will last a lifetime. To celebrate your purchase, make a redwork scissors keeper to keep them in and a little alphabet tag to identify who they belong to.

For how to embroider the Scissors heart design see Redwork Quilts: Embroidering the Heart Designs.

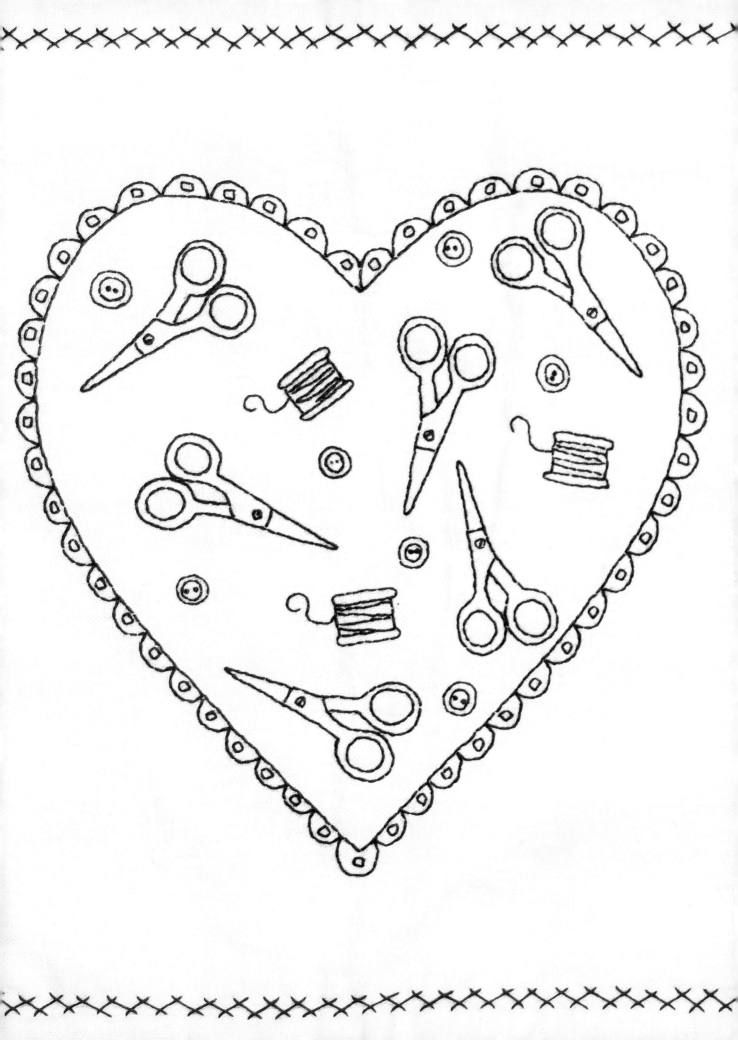

SCISSORS PROJECTS:
Scissors Keeper & Alphabet Tags

This really useful scissors keeper can be hung around your neck to ensure you don't lose your scissors down the back of the sofa! Quick and easy to make from offcuts of your favourite fabric, it is not only practical, but also beautiful when decorated with a touch of redwork embroidery. To make sure that everyone knows that these are your scissors, make a tag with your initial embroidered on it. This is a very simple and attractive way of marking your belongings, including your favourite scissors.

Scissors Keeper

YOU WILL NEED

20 x 15cm (8 x 6in) white linen main fabric

20 x 15cm (8 x 6in) red dot lining fabric

One skein of DMC 815 coton à broder no. 16

1m (1¼yd) 5mm (¼in) wide ribbon

Two small decorative buttons (optional)

FINISHED SIZE

18 x 7.5cm (7 x 3in)

STITCHES USED

Backstitch

Running stitch

TO MAKE THE SCISSORS KEEPER

1. Using the scissors keeper pattern (see Templates and Motifs), cut one from the red dot lining fabric and one from the white linen main fabric taking care to match the direction of the grain.

2. Mark the scissors motif onto the linen fabric, using your preferred method (see Transferring the Designs), centring the motif approx 2.5cm (1in) beneath the 'cleavage'. Embroider the scissors motif with backstitch.

3. Take the ribbon and pin it onto the right side of the linen as indicated on the pattern, so that the raw ends of the ribbon overlap the top curved edge by about 1cm (⅜in).

4. Place the lining fabric on top of the linen fabric with right sides together and pin along top curved edges (Fig. 1). Sew together with a scant 6mm (¼in) seam. Carefully snip the 'V' of the cleavage as indicated on the template.

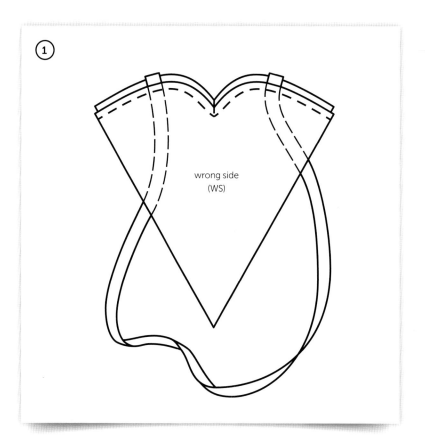

wrong side (WS)

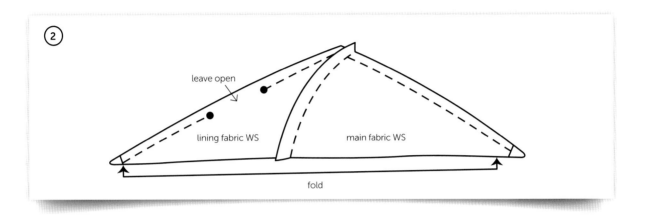

②

leave open

lining fabric WS   main fabric WS

fold

5. Open out the joined fabric and refold with right sides together along its length. Pin the centre seams, ensuring that they match, and pin along the entire length. Making sure that the ribbon strap is neatly tucked in and out of the way of any seams, sew along the outer edge seam, leaving a gap in the red dot lining fabric (see pattern and Fig. 2). Trim the points.

6. Turn to the right side through the opening in the lining fabric, and slip stitch the opening closed. Push the red dot lining into the linen fabric.

7. Sew a running stitch border along the top edge of the scissors keeper, and add two small decorative buttons to the outside edge of the strap.

Hang the scissors keeper around your neck and snip, snip, snip!

TIP

To make a scissors keeper for a larger (or smaller) pair of scissors, use the pattern and enlarge (or reduce) it on a photocopier.

Alphabet Tags

YOU WILL NEED

7.5 x 7.5cm (3 x 3in) white linen main fabric

7.5 x 7.5cm (3 x 3in) red dot backing fabric

One skein of DMC 815 coton à broder no. 16

5 x 10cm (2 x 4in) wadding (batting)

5 x 10cm (2 x 4in) cardboard

40cm (16in) baker's twine or thin ribbon

FINISHED SIZE

5cm (2in) diameter

STITCHES USED

Backstitch

Cross stitch

TO MAKE THE ALPHABET TAGS

1. Take the square of white linen fabric and transfer the initial of your choice (see Templates and Motifs: Alphabet Hanging) onto it using your preferred method (see Transferring the Designs). Stitch the design in backstitch; if you wish, you can fill the background with randomly spaced cross stitches as I have done on the 'm' alphabet tag.

2. Using the alphabet tags circle (see Templates and Motifs), cut two circles each from the card and the wadding (batting).

3. Pairing up a circle of card with a circle of wadding (batting), place the layered circles onto the back of the embroidered motif so that the wadding (batting) is lying against the wrong side of the redwork.

4. With doubled sewing thread and starting off with a knot, hand stitch a line of gathering (running) stitches around the outside edge of the redwork 6mm (¼in) in from the edge. Pull the gathers up tight around the cardboard and fasten off securely. Trim the excess fabric.

5. Repeat steps 3 and 4, this time gathering the backing fabric around the remaining card and wadding (batting) circles.

6. Place the fabric-gathered circles together with wrong sides facing. Fold the baker's twine in half and knot the ends. Working at the base of the circles, place the knotted end in between them to hide the knot.

7. Making sure that the looped cord is protruding from the bottom of the circles, ladder stitch them together (see Get Ready to Stitch).

8. Separate the cord loop to wrap each length around the edge of the circle, slip stitching in place securely as you go. Stitch the lengths together firmly at the top of the tag where they meet. You will now have a cord-trimmed circle and a loop for hanging.

Thread the cord loop over one of the handles of the scissors, slip the alphabet tag through the loop and proudly display your ownership!

TIP

These tags can be made using alphabets or a motif of your choosing from the additional motifs (see Templates and Motifs), or create a design of your own (see Design Your Own Motifs).

Stitch Motif:
Key

We have a beautiful collection of old keys hanging up in a corner of our house. The locks they opened have long been forgotten, but I often wonder what they once protected. It was the Ancient Egyptians, some 6,000 years ago, who first invented a lock and key made from wood. Their designs were improved by the Ancient Romans, who made the skeleton key, which we still have today. The flat key was invented in the 1800s and, although the modern world now has magnetic and digital locks, the little metal key will continue to be a symbol loaded with meaning. I used this motif to decorate the opening flap of my little sewing purse as it unlocks my very favourite things – my embroidery essentials!

For how to embroider the Key heart design see Redwork Quilts: Embroidering the Heart Designs.

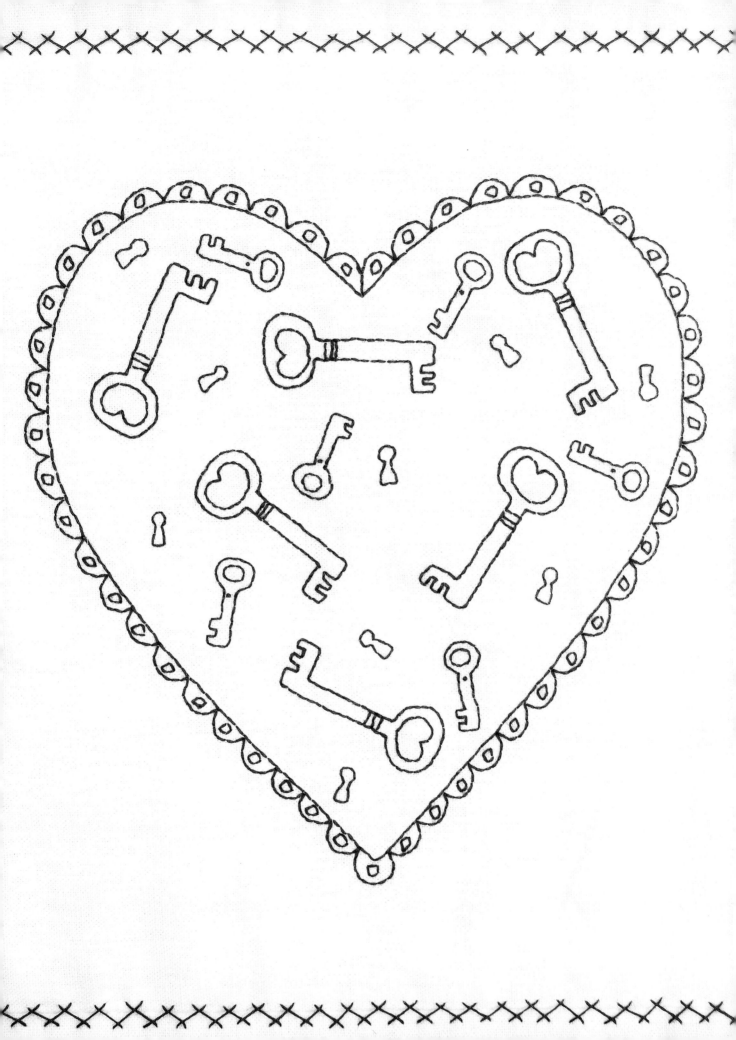

KEY PROJECT:

Sewing Purse

If, like me, you like to sit of an evening watching TV as you indulge in your embroidery, this little purse, designed to be worn around the neck, will prove indispensable. In fact, I created it to help improve family relations: no longer will the plot of the movie be lost along with my scissors, needle or thread! The redwork embroidered heart fastener is a reminder that the key to our hearts is a little sewing time.

Sewing Purse

YOU WILL NEED

23 x 28cm (9 x 11in) red star main fabric

23 x 28cm (9 x 11in) red check lining fabric

10 x 7.5cm (4 x 3in) white felt

7.5 x 7.5cm (3 x 3in) red felt

One skein of DMC 815 coton à broder no. 16

23 x 28cm (9 x 11in) cotton wadding (batting)

6.5 x 7.5cm (2½ x 3in) thick interfacing

80cm (32in) of approx 1cm (½in) wide tape

One popper (press stud)

Small amount of polyester toy filling

Two small pearl buttons

13cm (5in) baker's twine

Sewing thread to match main and lining fabrics

FINISHED SIZE

10 x 12.5cm (4 x 5in) closed

STITCHES USED

Backstitch

Blanket stitch

TO MAKE THE SEWING PURSE

1. Photocopy or trace the sewing purse pattern (see Templates and Motifs), transferring all the markings to use as a guide to positioning and assembly later. Use the paper pattern to cut out one lining fabric piece, one main fabric piece and one wadding (batting) piece.

2. Setting aside the main fabric sewing purse piece for the time being, lightly spray the wadding (batting) with spray adhesive following the manufacturer's instructions, and then attach it to the lining fabric.

3. From the remaining red star fabric, cut one piece measuring 7.5cm x 15cm (3 x 6in) and one piece 11.5 x 7.5cm (4½ x 3in). Cut a piece measuring 5 x 2.5cm (2 x 1in) from the red felt. These pieces will be used to make the heart-shaped scissors pocket, rectangular pocket and needle keeper on the lining of the sewing purse.

4. Take your wadding- (batting-) backed lining fabric and, using the pattern as a guide, pin the small red felt rectangle (needle keeper) in place and then stitch through both layers.

5. To make the scissors pocket, trace off the heart from the sewing purse pattern and transfer onto paper. Do **not** cut it out. Fold the 7.5cm x 15cm (3 x 6in) red star rectangle in half, right sides together so that the short edges meet. Pin the paper onto the fabric and stitch all the way around the heart using a very small stitch, leaving no gaps. Tear the paper off – this will be easy to do as the small stitches are like perforations.

6. Cut out the heart 3mm (⅛in) away from the stitching line and snip into the 'cleavage'. To make a turning gap, cut a small slit through one layer of fabric only (see pattern) and turn the heart the right way out. Pick out the curves of the heart so you have a nice shape (a wooden coffee stirring stick is ideal for this) and press. Using a matching thread topstitch close to the edge of the heart, from dot to dot as marked on the pattern. Now pin and sew the scissors pocket in place as marked on the pattern, again stitching from dot to dot.

7. Fold the remaining red star rectangle in half, wrong sides together and sew down both short sides with a 6mm (¼in) seam allowance; snip off the corners, turn right way out and press. To sew the prepared rectangular pocket in place, take the lining of the sewing purse and place in front of you so that the heart pocket is upside down. Position the raw edges of the pocket approx 2cm (¾in) up from the dash-dot fold line and pin. Stitch approx 6mm (¼in) from the raw edge of the pocket, then fold up the fabric and topstitch along each side to form the pocket.

8. Take the main fabric sewing purse piece and place it on top of the lining fabric, wrong sides facing, taking care to align the edges. Pin well, then machine stitch together all the way around the outer edge with a 6mm (¼in) seam, working very accurately and leaving an opening as indicated on the pattern. Snip off the corners, trim the curves and turn through to the right side. Press, picking out each seam so you have an accurate shape. Stitch the opening closed.

9. Mark the dash-dot fold lines with a disappearing pen onto the lining fabric side. Machine stitch along all the marked lines making sure to use a thread to match the lining fabric. Press all the fold lines well so that they will stay in place.

10. Fold the purse so that the right sides of the main fabric are together and match the side seams A to A and B to B, and oversew by hand. Turn the purse back through so that the right sides of the lining fabric are together and press once more.

11. To make the sewing purse strap, take your length of tape, turn under the ends and pin in position on the back of the purse (see pattern); hand sew in place.

12. To make the decorative heart fastener for the sewing purse flap, use the heart fastener pattern (see Templates and Motifs) to cut out two hearts from the white felt and one heart from the thick interfacing. Trim the interfacing so that it is slightly smaller than the felt hearts. Transfer the key design to one of the felt hearts and backstitch the design using coton à broder.

13. Once the embroidery is complete, layer up the hearts so that the interfacing heart is sandwiched between the white felt hearts with the embroidered heart positioned on top. Blanket stitch the hearts together, again using coton à broder.

14. Referring to the finished photograph, sew the top half of the heart onto the top of the purse flap using ladder stitch (see Get Ready to Stitch). Sew one half of the popper (press stud) beneath the white felt heart at the bottom edge, and the other half to the front of the purse, checking the closure before stitching in place.

15. To make a scissors keeper for a small pair of scissors, cut out two small hearts from red felt and sew together with blanket stitch, leaving a small gap to add a little toy filling. Before stitching the opening closed, take the baker's twine, fold in half and knot the ends; tuck the knot into the opening before continuing the blanket stitch. Sew on one small pearl button to the centre of the small red felt heart and one to the centre of the scissors pocket for decoration.

Attach the scissors keeper to your scissors, slip them into the pocket, shut the purse, and pop into your bag for stitching-on-the-go.

TIP

The scissors pocket is the perfect size to accommodate a 7.5cm (3in) pair of scissors.

Stitch Motif:
House

'And a house is not a home when there's no one there to hold you tight...'
Burt Bacharach, *A House is not a Home*

We have been decorating our homes since time began – just look at prehistoric cave paintings and the very earliest of pottery fragments decorated with thumb prints, animal hides, leather and woven cloth. There seems to be something deep within us that makes us cocoon ourselves in our homes, not only to protect those we care for most, but also to express to others who we are. I have overdosed on these home-making skills and there isn't an inch of our house undecorated by handmade lovelies. For this Englishwoman, her home is her castle. As it is easier to be lost than found, I have made a key tidy for my house key.

For how to embroider the House heart design see Redwork Quilts: Embroidering the Heart Designs.

HOUSE PROJECT:

Key Tidy

I dream of the day when I am organized and everything is in its right place. These simple little key tidies are a step in the right direction and they have the bonus of looking great. For the stopper bead, I used a small cotton reel I found in my stash but any type of bead will do to keep the key in place.

Key Tidy

YOU WILL NEED

15 x 10cm (6 x 4in) main fabric

15 x 10cm (6 x 4in) red star lining fabric

7.5 x 5cm (3 x 2in) white linen fabric

One skein of DMC 321 coton à broder no. 16

White sewing thread

30cm (12in) cord

6mm (¼in) bead

1.3cm (½in) mini cotton reel

7.5 x 5cm (3 x 2in) cardboard

Split ring or trigger clasp for attaching key

Spray starch

FINISHED SIZE

9 x 6.5cm (3¹/₂ x 2¹/₂in)

STITCHES USED

Backstitch

French knot

TO MAKE THE KEY TIDY

1. Using the key tidy pattern provided (see Templates and Motifs), cut two from your lining fabric and two from your main fabric. Use the oval template to cut one from card and one 1.3cm (½in) bigger all around from the white linen fabric.

2. Transfer a house design, or a motif of your choosing, onto the white linen oval using your preferred method (see Transferring the Designs). Embroider the motif with backstitch using coton à broder. Work a French knot for the door handle.

3. With doubled sewing thread and starting off with a knot, hand stitch a line of gathering (running) stitches approx 1.3cm (½in) in from the outside edge of the redwork oval. Pull the gathers up tight around the cardboard and fasten off securely. Give the gathered redwork oval a spray starch and a good press before removing the card.

TIP

Make a key tidy for each of your keys choosing a motif that will help you pick up the right key at a glance: shed, car, beach hut, house.

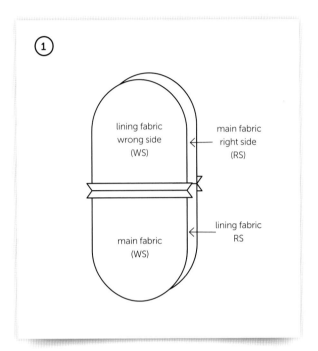

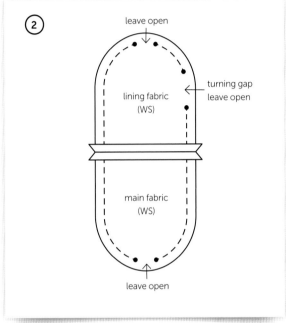

4. Place the redwork oval (right side facing up) onto the right side of the front of the key tidy; pin, then blanket stitch in place.

5. Place the key tidy front right sides together with one of the lining fabric pieces and sew along the straight edge only. Press the seam open.

6. Repeat step 5 to join the key tidy back to the remaining lining fabric piece.

7. Put the joined main fabric/lining fabric pieces together with right sides facing, placing them so that the main fabric lines up with the lining fabric (see Fig. 1); pin well at the side seam.

8. Sew the pinned pieces together with a smaller than normal stitch, leaving a turning gap on the side of one of the linings and a much smaller opening at the mid-point of each curve for threading through the cord in step 10 (see Fig. 2).

9. Trim the curved seams and turn the key tidy the right way out through its turning gap. Stitch this opening closed, then push the lining up into the key tidy, allowing the lining to overlap on the bottom straight edge by 6mm (¼in). Press.

10. Thread the bead onto your cord until it is halfway along the length. Fold the cord in half and tie an

overhand knot beneath it. Now thread the ends through the mini cotton reel and into the small opening on the curved edge, taking care to ease it through the gaps in both the main and the lining fabric. Knot the threads onto a split ring or trigger clasp, and attach the ring or clasp to your key.

Pull up the cord to make the key disappear inside the key tidy. Magic!

TIP

A pair of tweezers is useful to help to pull the cord through the small openings at the top of the key tidy.

Stitch Motif:

Daisy

Bees are under threat like never before and it seems that this may be partly due to the reduction in the abundance of wild flowers in the countryside. Bees need flowers throughout spring and summer to provide pollen and nectar, and the best plants for this are cottage garden flowers and native species. The humble daisy is, in fact, the ideal flower. So let the daisies grow in your garden and wear this pretty daisy brooch with pride, and who knows – you might attract a bumblebee or two.

For how to embroider the Daisy heart design see Redwork Quilts: Embroidering the Heart Designs.

DAISY PROJECT:
Daisy Brooch

I love wearing handmade jewellery and this simple little brooch is no exception. It can be made in a couple of hours and is perfect for using up small scraps of linen and leftover lengths of thread.

Daisy Brooch

YOU WILL NEED

7.5 x 7.5cm (3 x 3in) white linen main fabric

Two pieces of backing fabric each measuring 6.5cm x 9cm (2¹/₂ x 3¹/₂in)

DMC 815 coton à broder no. 16

7.5 x 7.5cm (3 x 3in) wadding (batting)

7.5 x 7.5cm (3 x 3in) medium-weight interfacing

Brooch back

FINISHED SIZE

Approx 6.5cm (2¹/₂in) diameter

STITCHES USED

Backstitch

TO MAKE THE DAISY BROOCH

1. Transfer the daisy brooch design (see Templates and Motifs) onto the square of linen fabric using your preferred method (see Transferring the Designs).

2. Attach the wadding (batting) square to the back of the linen by lightly spraying with spray adhesive, following the manufacturer's instructions, or tack (baste) in place.

TIP

The back of the brooch is made as described in step 4 so that you can insert the interfacing/wadding (batting) in step 8, which will help to keep a nice firm shape.

3. Backstitch the daisy brooch design with the coton à broder.

4. Take your two pieces of backing fabric and turn under a small hem on the long edges of each, sewing them in place by hand or by machine. Overlap the hemmed edges by 1.3cm (½in) and pin.

5. Place the backing fabric square and the redwork linen square together with right sides facing. Sew around the outside edge of the redwork design using a very small stitch. Trim the seam allowance to 3mm (⅛in).

6. Turn the brooch the right way out via the overlapped seams and use a wooden stick to smooth out the seam for a nice, neat finish.

7. To create the ridge at the edge of the brooch, hand sew a construction running stitch on the inside circle on top of the backstitch line.

8. Cut a circle from both the interfacing and the wadding (batting), using the inside circle of the daisy brooch design as a guide. Layer one on top of the other and place into the opening at the back of the brooch, then oversew the opening closed.

Sew a brooch back onto the back of the brooch and wear it with pride.

Stitch Motif:
Hand

  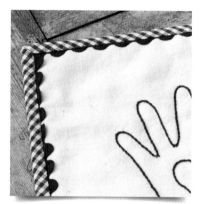

The open hand is a universal symbol of protection warding off evil. It can be traced back to the Ancient Egyptians and it has evolved to become a sacred and respected talisman in many religions and cultures. The open-handed palm can also bestow fertility, good luck and good health. For me, it is the image of holding hands that particularly appeals, as a sign of protection, guidance, love, care and friendship. The hand motif is a great way to personalize your table linens for family meals.

For how to embroider the Hand heart design see Redwork Quilts: Embroidering the Heart Designs.

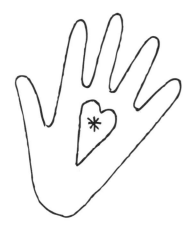

HAND PROJECT:
Little Hands Place Mat

The beautiful little chubby hands that are embroidered on the place mat are taken from the handprints of my grandson, Bertie. Children love to make handprint paintings to adorn your kitchen cupboards, and now you can preserve these precious mementoes of childhood by stitching them onto a place mat or wall hanging. What a wonderful gift for doting parents, or even grandparents!

Little Hands Place Mat

YOU WILL NEED

32 x 21.5cm (12$\frac{1}{2}$ x 8$\frac{1}{2}$in) white linen/cotton mix main fabric

37 x 27cm (14$\frac{1}{2}$ x 10$\frac{1}{2}$in) red dot backing fabric

37 x 27cm (14$\frac{1}{2}$ x 10$\frac{1}{2}$in) cotton wadding (batting)

One skein of DMC 321 coton à broder no. 16

1m (42in) of 18mm (1$\frac{1}{16}$in) wide red check ready-made bias binding

1m (42in) of wide red ric-rac

FINISHED SIZE

32 x 21.5cm (12$\frac{1}{2}$ x 8$\frac{1}{2}$in)

STITCHES USED

Stem stitch

TO MAKE THE PLACE MAT

1. Draw around your child's hands with a pencil, then neaten the lines up with a black felt-tip pen. Transfer your child's hand motifs onto white linen/cotton mix fabric using your preferred method (see Transferring the Designs), placing them so that the thumbs are at least 1cm (⅜in) apart. Transfer a heart motif to the middle of each of the hands and the initial of your child's first name beneath the hands (see Templates and Motifs).

2. Attach the wadding (batting) to the back of the linen by lightly spraying with spray adhesive, following the manufacturer's instructions, and making sure that the linen fabric is centralized on the wadding (batting).

3. Embroider the design with coton à broder and your favourite redwork stitch – this time I used stem stitch.

4. Once your embroidery is complete, lightly spray the back of the wadding (batting) with spray adhesive and smooth the backing fabric onto it, trimming if necessary. Tack (baste) all the way around the edges.

5. Cut four pieces of ric-rac, two measuring 32cm (12½in) and two measuring 21.5cm (8½in). Pin the longer pieces of ric-rac to the top and bottom edge of the place mat, making sure to align the humps with the raw edge of the fabric. Tack (baste) through the middle of the ric-rac, and repeat to attach the shorter lengths to the side edges.

6. Apply the ready-made binding (see Polar Bear Project: Cake Band), then remove the tacking (basting) stitches. Press well.

Set the table and cut the cake!

TIP

If you prefer, you can use a pair of hands from the Hand heart motif, enlarging them to child or adult size as you desire.

Stitch Motif:

Holly

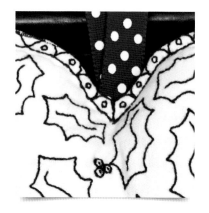  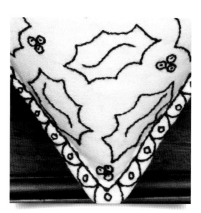

The holly plant brings to mind all I love most about winter – warm fires, bright berries and robin red breast. In pre-Victorian times 'Christmas tree' meant holly bushes. Christian symbolism connected it to the crown of thorns. The holly bush is surrounded in myth and legend, and it was also thought to have protective properties, so I have made a holly heart for you to hang above your front door, to welcome visitors and to protect your home this winter.

For how to embroider the Holly heart design see Redwork Quilts: Embroidering the Heart Designs.

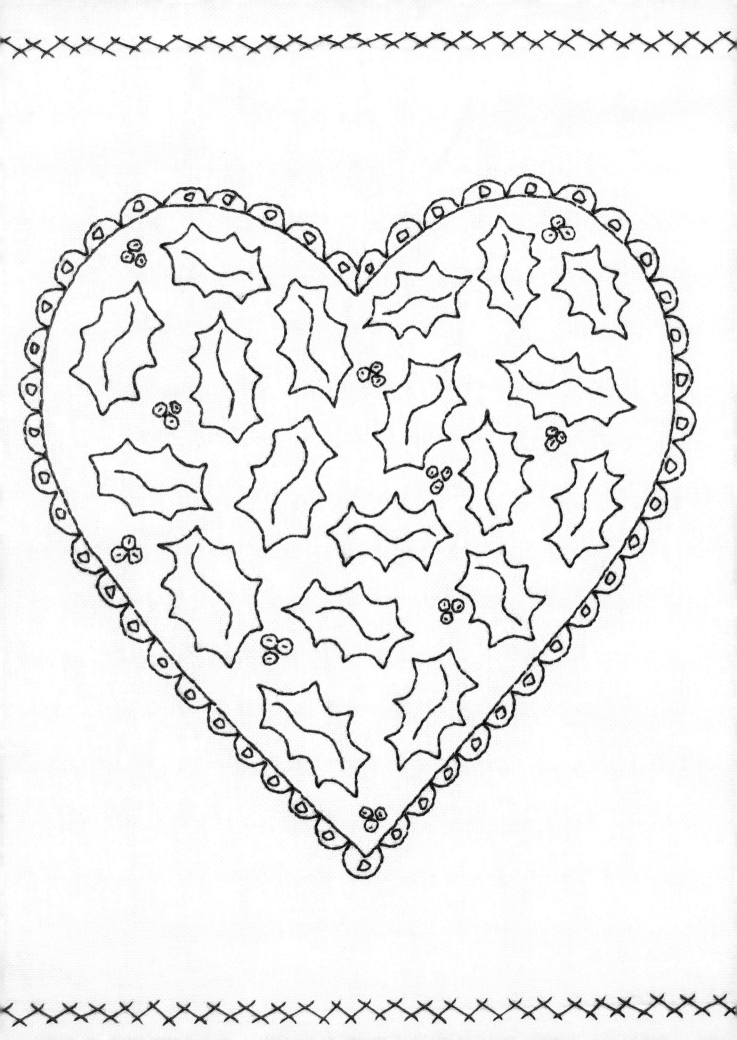

HOLLY PROJECT:
Hanging Heart

These hanging hearts are great not only for decorating your home, but also to give as gifts. They are simple to make but do include an unusual technique for creating an opening for turning and stuffing, so follow the instructions carefully and all will be fine! The holly heart design makes this the perfect decoration for Christmas, but any of the heart designs can be used for the project. Or you can trace off the heart border design and fill it with a selection of your favourite motifs from the Templates section, or with a design of your very own making.

Hanging Heart

YOU WILL NEED

25 x 25cm (10 x 10in) white linen main fabric

25 x 25cm (10 x 10in) red check backing fabric

One skein of DMC 815 coton à broder no. 16

25 x 25cm (10 x 10in) iron-on lightweight interfacing

Small bag of polyester toy filling

1m (1yd) of 1.5cm (⁵⁄₈in) wide ribbon

FINISHED SIZE

20 x 20cm (8 x 8in)

STITCHES USED

Backstitch

TO MAKE THE HANGING HEART

1. Transfer the holly heart design (see Templates and Motifs), or a pattern of your choosing, onto the linen square using your preferred method (see Transferring the Designs).

2. Iron the interfacing to the wrong side of the linen. This will stabilize the fabric and prevent stray threads from showing on the right side.

3. Embroider your chosen motif using coton à broder. The whole of the holly heart, including the scalloped border, was stitched using backstitch, with single stitches worked inside the holly berries. Press the finished embroidery.

4. Pin the embroidered fabric and the backing fabric together with right sides facing. Machine stitch, or use hand backstitch, to sew the two pieces together, 6mm (¼in) from the outside edge of the embroidered scalloped border. Be sure to sew all the way around leaving no gap.

TIP

For a great nursery decoration, fill a heart with some letters from the alphabet (see Templates and Motifs), and include the letters of your child's name, so that they can start to pick them out.

1

slit for turning/stuffing

backing fabric
wrong side

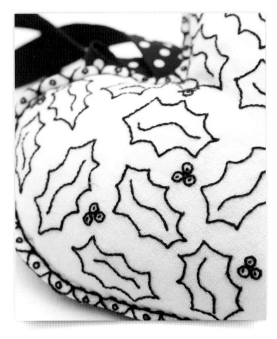

5. Trim the heart shape 6mm (¼in) from the sewn edge. Snip across the point at the bottom of the heart and snip into the heart's 'cleavage' at the top of the heart. This ensures that a nice shape is achieved when the heart is stuffed.

6. Working on the back of the heart, cut a horizontal line 4cm (1½in) across, approx 4cm (1½in) down from the top of the heart through one layer of fabric only, to create a gap large enough for you to stuff the heart in a little while (see Fig. 1).

7. Carefully turn the heart through to the right side through the slit. To make the decorative edge of the heart, go over the backstitch of this shape (the inside line of the scallops) with the coton à broder working through both fabric layers.

8. Stuff the heart firmly with toy filling easing it through the slit, then ladder stitch the opening closed (see Get Ready to Stitch).

9. To make the hanging loop, start by cutting the ribbon in two. Take one piece of ribbon, fold it in half and slightly cross it over halfway down; stitch in place onto the heart over the slit. Tie a bow in the other half of the ribbon and stitch in place also over the slit.

Your hanging heart is ready to be hung – let the celebrations begin!

TIP

Sewing up a turning gap once stuffing is completed always leaves a crooked seam, so the discreet turning/stuffing slit technique avoids creating an untidy seam. When cutting the slit, you need to be careful not to cut through both layers, so do make sure you just pick up the one layer before you snip.

Stitch Motif:

Dove

The symbol of a dove has been used for centuries in all forms of artwork across the world. Doves mate for life, are incredibly loyal and work hard together to raise their family. Perhaps this is why they are used as a universal symbol for love, peace and hope. Make yourself a little flying dove and hang it where you will see it each day to remember these positive attributes.

For how to embroider the Dove heart design see Redwork Quilts: Embroidering the Heart Designs.

DOVE PROJECT:
Flying Dove

These little doves are incredibly easy to make and, while they look lovely on their own, as doves mate for life, I think a pair is necessary. Once they are made, hang them up somewhere in your home so they can look after you and your family. This project is suitable to sew with young children.

Flying Dove

YOU WILL NEED

20 x 20cm (8 x 8in) white felt

2.5 x 2.5cm (1 x 1in) black felt

One skein of DMC 815 coton à broder no. 16

Handful of polyester toy filling

Black embroidery thread

Fabric glue

FINISHED SIZE

7.5 x 5cm (3 x 2in)

STITCHES USED

Blanket stitch

French knot

TO MAKE THE FLYING DOVE

1. Trace the dove patterns (see Templates and Motifs) onto paper and cut out to give you your pattern pieces. Using the patterns, cut out the following pieces: from the white felt, two bodies, one gusset and four wings; from the black felt, one beak.

2. Place the body pieces together and hand sew around the top edge only using coton à broder and blanket stitch, starting at the dot just below the head and finishing at the dot at the tail (see pattern), leaving a small opening as marked on the pattern to pop the beak in later.

3. Take the gusset and insert it in between the partially joined body pieces as marked on the pattern. Pin and then sew with blanket stitch along one side from dot to dot, and then along the other side, this time leaving a small stuffing gap.

4. Gently stuff the body with your toy filling, paying particular attention to the head and tail. Sew the opening closed with blanket stitch.

5. Pair up the wings and sew each pair together with blanket stitch (no stuffing is required). Use fabric glue to attach the wings to either side of the body.

6. To give the dove eyes, sew a French knot using black thread to each side of the head as indicated on the pattern.

7. Take the black felt beak piece and fold in half as marked on the pattern. Use black embroidery thread to oversew along the edge. Pop the beak into the opening left in the dove's head (see step 2), pushing in the end so that only the triangular shape is visible. Sew in place.

Sew a little ribbon to the back of the dove to hang it up and let it fly.

TIP

The flying dove can be used to celebrate a number of occasions – Valentine's Day and engagements, weddings and wedding anniversaries, and Christmas, of course. But why wait for a celebration? If you want to fill your home with love and peace, display your dove all year long.

Redwork
Quilts

Inspired by the vintage penny square redwork quilt that I found on an antique stand at a quilt show, I have used my redwork heart designs to make two fabulous quilts, one using all nine of the designs and the other combining a few with nine-patch patchwork blocks.

So first let me introduce the redwork hearts quilt. At first glance it may look a little daunting, but please be reassured it is not. Reminiscent of the penny square quilt (see History of Redwork), each heart design is embroidered as an individual square. Once all nine squares have been embroidered, simply sew them together. I have added a simple border, embroidered with nine smaller single-motif hearts. Then there is the nine-patch redwork hearts quilt, which has fewer embroidered blocks combined with four nine-patch patchwork blocks, finished with a simple patchwork border.

Redwork Hearts Quilt

YOU WILL NEED

1.25m (50in) of 150cm (60in) wide white linen fabric for the quilt top

112 x 112cm (44 x 44in) red dot fabric for backing

23cm (9in) of 107cm (42in) wide red dot fabric for binding

112 x 112cm (44 x 44in) thin cotton mix wadding (batting)

1.25m (50in) white lightweight iron-on interfacing

18 skeins of DMC 815 coton à broder no. 16

200 safety pins or one can of spray adhesive

FINISHED SIZE

Approx 101.5 x 101.5cm (40 x 40in)

STITCHES USED

Backstitch

Running stitch

Herringbone stitch

French knot

Cross stitch

TO MAKE THE REDWORK HEARTS QUILT

1. From the white linen fabric and the iron-on interfacing, cut the following pieces:

Nine 27 x 27cm (10½ x 10½in) squares for the embroidered heart designs;

Two 14 x 78cm (5½ x 30½in) strips for the side borders;

Two 14 x 103cm (5½ x 40½in) strips for the top and bottom borders.

2. Working each of the nine embroidery squares one at a time, transfer each of the redwork heart designs (see Embroidering the Heart Designs) onto the middle of the linen squares using your preferred method (see Transferring the Designs).

3. Fuse the iron-on interfacing squares to the wrong side of your prepared fabric squares and embroider the designs using coton à broder (see Embroidering the Heart Designs for full details).

4. Following the finished quilt photograph as a guide, transfer the small heart design (see Templates and Motifs) onto the side, top and bottom borders, and fill each with one single motif from the heart designs. Fuse the iron-on interfacing strips to the wrong side of your prepared border strips before embroidering the designs.

5. Press the embroidered linen fabric squares and lay them out in three rows of three, following the layout in the photograph or rearranging them as you prefer. Pin the squares in each row together easing any fullness evenly across each square. Sew the squares together with a 6mm (¼in) seam allowance. Press seams open.

6. Attach the borders to the top and bottom of the embroidered squares panel first: pin in place, then sew on using a 6mm (¼in) seam allowance; press the seams open. Now attach the side borders in the same way. Give the quilt top a final press.

7. Following the advice in Quilt-Making Techniques: Preparation for Quilting, make a quilt sandwich in preparation for quilting.

8. First, to stabilize the layered quilt, machine stitch-in-the-ditch around each block and along the borders, using an invisible or matching thread. Then decorate by working a herringbone stitch border around the seam lines of the embroidered squares using coton à broder. At first you may find it difficult to get an even stitch but eventually a nice rhythm will develop and as it gathers pace, the stitch will become easier to sew.

9. Finally bind the quilt – see Quilt-Making Techniques: Double Binding.

TIP

If you prefer, you can substitute the motifs in the heart designs for those of your own choosing. Simply trace the large heart design onto your square and fill with your preferred motifs, positioning them in a random manner. For stitching on-the-go, pop one in your project bag and grab your sewing purse.

Nine-Patch Redwork Hearts Quilt

YOU WILL NEED

1m (40in) of 150cm (60in) wide white linen fabric for the quilt top

50cm (20in) of 150cm (60in) wide red dot fabric for patchwork and borders

30cm (12in) of 107cm (42in) wide red dot fabric for binding

107cm (42in) of 107cm (42in) wide red dot fabric for backing

Five skeins of DMC 815 coton à broder no. 16

107 x 107cm (42 x 42in) cotton/polyester mix wadding (batting)

50cm (20in) white lightweight iron-on interfacing

200 safety pins or one can of spray adhesive

Matching sewing thread

36 small red buttons

4m (4³/₈yd) of wide red ric-rac

Creative grids 7.5cm (3in) wavy border ruler

FINISHED SIZE

Approx 99 x 99cm (39 x 39in)

STITCHES USED

This will depend on the five heart designs you choose. For the full list of stitches used in the nine heart designs, see Redwork Hearts Quilt.

TO MAKE THE NINE-PATCH REDWORK HEARTS QUILT QUILT

1. From the white linen fabric, cut the following pieces:

Five 24 x 24cm (9½ x 9½in) squares for the embroidered heart designs

One 9 x 72cm (3½ x 28in) strip and two 9 x 36cm (3½ x 14in) strips for the nine-patch blocks

Twenty 9 x 9cm (3½ x 3½in) squares for the patchwork border

Two 9 x 85cm (3½ x 33½in) strips for top and bottom borders

Two 9 x 100cm (3½ x 39½in) strips for the side borders

2. From the red dot fabric, cut the following pieces:

One 9 x 36cm (3½ x 14in) strip and two 9 x 72cm (3½ x 28in) strips for the nine-patch blocks

Twenty 9 x 9cm (3½ x 3½in) squares for the patchwork border

3. From the iron-on interfacing, cut the following pieces:

Five 24 x 24cm (9½ x 9½in) squares for the embroidered heart designs

4. Choose five of the redwork designs (see Embroidering the Heart Designs) and transfer your chosen designs onto the middle of the 24 x 24cm (9½ x 9½in) linen squares using your preferred method (see Transferring the Designs).

5. Fuse the iron-on interfacing squares to the wrong side of your prepared fabric squares and embroider the designs using coton à broder (see Embroidering the Heart Designs for full details).

6. To make the nine-patch blocks, start by taking the two long red dot strips and sew them to either side of the long 9 x 71cm (3½ x 28in) white strip. Sew the strips together carefully using a 6mm (¼in) seam allowance. Press the seams away from the middle. Very carefully, cut up the joined-together strips into eight sections each measuring 9cm (3½in) – see Fig. 1.

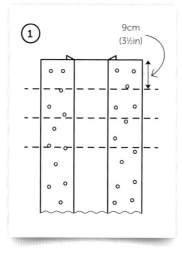

TIP

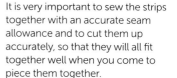

It is very important to sew the strips together with an accurate seam allowance and to cut them up accurately, so that they will all fit together well when you come to piece them together.

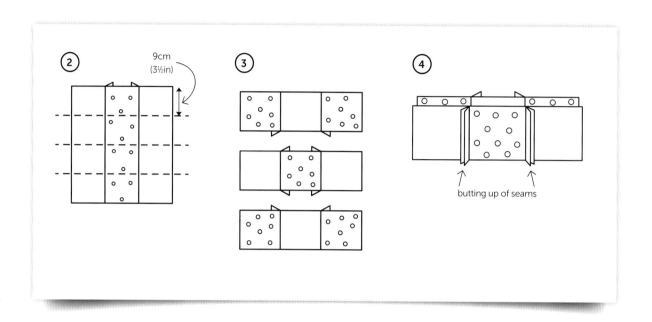

9cm
(3½in)

② ③ ④

butting up of seams

7. Take the two short white strips and sew them to either side of the remaining red dot strip. Again, sew the strips together carefully using a 6mm (¼in) seam allowance, but this time press the seams **towards** the middle (see Fig. 2). Very carefully, cut up the joined-together strips into four sections each measuring 9cm (3½in).

8. Take two red/white/red strips and one white/red/white strip (Fig. 3), and sew them together with an accurate 6mm (¼in) seam allowance so that the white/red/white strip is in the middle, to make one complete nine-patch block. When joining the strips, butt up the seam allowances (see Fig. 4). Press. Make four of these blocks in all.

9. Join the nine-patch and redwork squares together in three rows, referring to the centre panel of Fig. 5 as your guide. The first row is a redwork block joined to a nine-patch, joined to another redwork block; the second row is a nine-patch block joined to a redwork block, joined to another redwork block; and the third row is a repeat of row 1. When joining

the blocks use a neat and accurate 6mm (¼in) seam; once all the blocks in the row are joined together, press seams open.

10. Now join the three rows of blocks together, matching the seams carefully. Pin the seams that match together and ease the rest of the fabric in. Sew the rows together with a 6mm (¼in) seam and press.

11. To make the inner (patchwork) border, join the 9 x 9cm (3½ x 3½in) red dot and white squares alternately into strips, using a 6mm (¼in) seam allowance as follows: make two strips by sewing five red and four white squares together, starting with a red; make two strips by sewing six white and five red squares together, starting with a white square. Press all seams open.

12. Carefully join the two shorter strips to the top and bottom of the quilt matching seams and pinning them as you go, taking care to match the border seams with the nine-patch block seams. Sew together with a 6mm (¼in) seam. Press seams open.

TIP

An accurate 6mm (¼in) seam allowance is so very important to make sure the borders will fit well. This is a very adaptable quilt that gives you the option of making a quilt that is a lot bigger in less time: for a larger quilt, you could combine eight embroidered heart squares with seven nine-patch blocks.

13. Sew the two longer strips to either side of the quilt in the same way, again paying careful attention to the matching of seams on the nine-patch blocks. Press.

14. Sew the outer border strips in place using a 6mm (¼in) seam allowance: take the shorter white fabric strips and join to the top and bottom of the quilt, press seams open, then join the longer white fabric strips to each side and press again.

15. I added a few (optional) embellishments to my quilt top. I sewed little red buttons in all the white squares. I used the Creative Grids ruler to mark the wavy line on the outer border of the quilt, pinning then sewing ric-rac on top of this line, machine stitching right through the middle of the braid.

16. Following the advice in Quilt-Making Techniques: Preparation for Quilting, make a quilt sandwich in preparation for quilting. When pinning the quilt layers together, do not forget to pin the borders as well. Once your quilt layers are securely joined, tack (baste) all the way around the border.

17. First, to stabilize the layered quilt, machine stitch-in-the-ditch around each block and along the borders, using an invisible or matching thread (see Quilt-Making Techniques: In-the-Ditch Quilting). I then machine quilted across the red dot fabric squares from corner to corner, to form a cross in each one; this is known as crosshatching.

18. Finally, bind the quilt – see Quilt-Making Techniques: Double Binding.

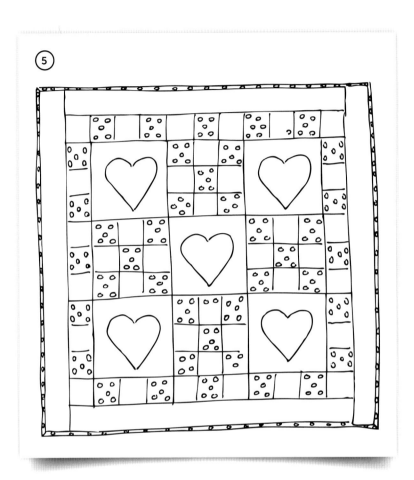

TIP

When stitching the ric-rac braid onto the quilt top, fit a walking foot to your machine. For a perfectly neat finish, once the ric-rac is sewn on, unpick a few stitches in a side seam and tuck in the raw ends of the ric-rac and hand stitch the opening closed.

TIP

While you can crosshatch quilt the red dot squares by eye, I prefer to use a blunt tapestry needle and a ruler in order to mark each square from corner to corner, with a light scratch of the needle to indent the fabric for a stitching guideline.

Embroidering the Heart Designs

Trace off the large heart design (see Templates and Motifs) and fill with the stitch motifs arranged to your liking, using the photographs of the finished heart designs as a guide (see Stitch Motif chapter openers). In fact, if you prefer, you can trace off the designs directly from these photographs as they are reproduced at actual size.

HEART

Embroider the motif outlines with backstitch, first the large heart and its border, and then the small motifs inside the large heart. Work a French knot for the dot at the top of each heart. For the stars, work a cross stitch then make another cross stitch on top at a different angle.

POLAR BEAR

Embroider the motif outlines with backstitch, first the large heart and its border, and then the small motifs inside the large heart. Work French knots for the bears' eyes and single stitches for their freckles.

SCISSORS

Embroider the motif outlines with backstitch, first the large heart and its border, and then the small motifs inside the large heart. Embroider small French knots for the buttonholes or sew using a tiny stitch.

KEY

Embroider the motif outlines with backstitch, first the large heart and its border, and then the small motifs inside the large heart.

HOUSE

Embroider the motif outlines with backstitch, first the large heart and its border, and then the small motifs inside the large heart. Work French knots for the door handles on all the houses and embroider a line of cross stitches on the cottage roofs.

DAISY

Embroider the motif outlines with backstitch, first the large heart and its border, and then the small motifs inside the large heart.

HAND

Embroider the motif outlines with backstitch, first the large heart and its border, and then the small motifs inside the large heart. Work a cross stitch on top of another cross stitch at a different angle to create a star stitch in the middle of each of the small hearts.

HOLLY

Embroider the motif outlines with backstitch, first the large heart and its border, and then the small motifs inside the large heart. Work a single stitch in each berry.

DOVE

Embroider the motif outlines with backstitch, first the large heart and its border, and then the small motifs inside the large heart. Work French knots for the doves' eyes and lines of running stitch for their breast feathers. The birds' footprints, are made with three long straight stitches worked at three different angles (see Stitch Motif: Dove chapter opener photograph).

Quilt-Making Techniques

PREPARING TO QUILT

It is often said that 'quilting makes the quilt' and preparation is key to your success; do not be tempted to rush this part, after all you do not want to spoil your work at this stage.

1. Prepare the quilt top for layering by pressing all seams and cutting off any stray threads.

2. Cut a piece of backing fabric and a piece of cotton wadding (batting) at least 5cm (2in) bigger all around than the quilt top.

3. Lay the backing fabric on a flat surface wrong side facing you; smooth it out. Secure the fabric to the surface with a low-tack tape, ensuring that it is perfectly flat and under a little tension. Lay the wadding (batting) on top and smooth it out flat. Finally, complete your quilt sandwich by placing the quilt top on top of the wadding (batting) and smooth it out.

4. Pin the layers of the quilt together, using safety pins every 7.5cm (3in). Start in the middle and work your way out to the edges. Do not scrimp on pins as this will lead to rucks and creases. Alternatively, use spray adhesive to keep your layers together, following the manufacturer's instruction and remembering to spray the wadding (batting) only, **not** the fabrics.

5. Tack (baste) around the outside edge of the quilt; trim the wadding (batting) and backing to match the quilt top.

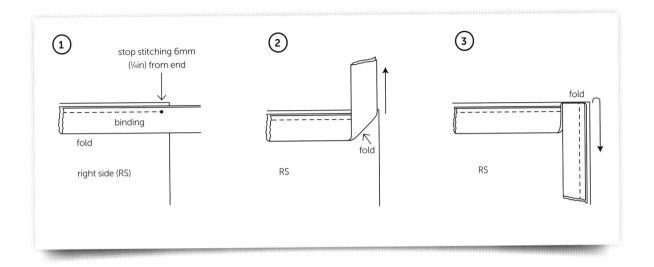

IN-THE-DITCH QUILTING

This is my favourite part as, for me, it is when the quilt comes to life. I tend to break all the rules, using both machine and hand quilting. I use the machine to stabilize the quilt so it does not move around, then hand stitches to give the quilt a homely handmade feel.

1. Once the quilt is nicely layered, quilt the blocks by sewing around all the squares in the seam line, or in-the-ditch as it is commonly known, remembering to stitch along the border strips too. Use an ordinary thread in a matching colour.

TIP

I always use a walking foot when machine quilting. This is not generally included in the box of accessories and will need to be purchased as an extra, but it is well worth it. The foot 'walks' across the quilt and its layers, and prevents puckering.

DOUBLE-BINDING

The first place a quilt will wear will be along the binding, so making your binding double thickness gives extra strength. It also provides an already neatened folded seam to slip stitch in place once the binding has been sewn on.

1. Cut four 7.5cm (3in) strips across the width of your fabric to make a binding and join to form one continuous length. Press open the seams. Press the strip in half with wrong sides together across the length.

2. Working with the right side of the quilt facing you, lay the binding along one side, matching the raw edges. Pin in place. (Only pin the binding to the side you are working on; when you have completed the mitre of the first corner, you can then pin the next side, and so on.)

3. Starting 15cm (6in) from the beginning of the binding, machine sew using a generous 6mm (¼in) seam. Stitch until you reach one corner, stopping exactly 6mm (¼in) from the end (Fig. 1).

4. Pull the work away from the machine and fold the binding up so that it is aligned with the edge of the quilt, making sure it is straight, as shown in Fig. 2.

5. Holding the corner, fold the binding back down, aligning it with the raw edge and making sure that the folded corner is square. Pin and sew over the fold continuing down the next side (Fig. 3).

6. Continue to bind around the remaining sides, following Figs. 1–3 at each corner. Stop stitching 15cm (6in) from the end. Lay both ends of the binding along the quilt's edge and fold them back where they meet. Finger press the folds well. Trim to 6mm (¼in) from the folded ends, and stitch together. Open out and finger press the seam. Complete the sewing of the binding along the edge.

7. Fold the binding over to the back of the quilt and slip stitch in place. The corners mitre beautifully on their own – all you need to do is slip stitch them closed.

Extra
Inspirations

People often ask me where I get my ideas and inspiration. The truth is that over the years I have collected a treasure trove of lovely things, from old children's books to vintage needlework magazines, from toys and china to antique locks and keys, and so many fabrics and buttons, of course. I collect from car boot sales as well as antique shops and fairs. These carefully chosen items adorn my shelves and fill my drawers, and inspire me to re-create them in my embroideries. In this chapter, I have two more projects to share with you – a simple little project bag inspired by a children's book illustration from my collection, and a delightful sampler offering borders and an alphabet for you to personalize your own projects – and, perhaps most important of all, the advice you will need to design your very own redwork motifs.

EXTRA PROJECT:

Project Bag

This lovely little bag is perfect for storing your redwork heart designs whilst in the making for stitching on the go. It's simple to make and you can adapt any small redwork design to fit in the 12.5cm (5in) square. For the embroidery, this time I used a finer thread, a wool Lana from Maderia, but two strands of stranded cotton (floss) would also work.

Project Bag

YOU WILL NEED

25cm (10in) of 42in wide denim main fabric

24 x 80cm (9¹/₂ x 31¹/₂in) red spot lining fabric

14 x 14cm (5¹/₂ x 5¹/₂in) white linen embroidery fabric

One skein of Maderia Lana red wool thread

15 x 15cm (6 x 6in) iron-on lightweight interfacing

56cm (22in) of medium red ric-rac

Bag handle

Small popper (press stud)

FINISHED SIZE

Approx 24 x 28cm (9¹/₂ x 11in) closed

STITCHES USED

Backstitch

Running stitch

TO MAKE THE PROJECT BAG

1. From the denim main fabric, cut the following:

One piece measuring 24 x 21.5cm (9½ x 8½in);

Two pieces measuring 6 x 14cm (2½ x 5½in);

One piece measuring 24 x 44.5cm (9½ x 17½in).

2. From the red dot lining fabric, cut one piece measuring 24 x 80cm (9½ x 31½in).

3. Take the square of white linen fabric and transfer the young girl sewing motif (see Templates and Motifs) onto it using your preferred method (see Transferring the Designs). Fuse the interfacing to the wrong side of the linen fabric and stitch the design in backstitch. Work a line of running stitch at the bottom of the girl's dress and also on the fabric she is holding, and stitch the facial features with small straight stitches. Once the embroidery is complete, press the work.

TIP

I love the shape of this bag and I feel it would make a great shoulder bag made from soft leather without the embroidered patch. I do urge you to experiment with your fabric choices – you will be surprised how different projects can look when made from different fabrics.

4. Cut the ric-rac into four equal pieces, each measuring approx 14cm (5½in). Sew a length of ric-rac to the top and bottom edges of the embroidered square while aligning the ric-rac edge to the raw edge of the work, and sewing through the middle of the braid. Repeat to attach the remaining two lengths to the sides of the embroidered square.

5. Sew the 6 x 14cm (2½ x 5½in) denim pieces to either side of the redwork square using the line that you sewed the ric-rac on as a guide to the seam allowance. Press the seams towards the denim. Sew the 24 x 21.5cm (9½ x 8½in) denim piece to the top of the redwork square in the same way, and again, press seams towards the denim. Finally, sew the remaining denim piece to the bottom of the redwork and press seams as before (see Fig. 1).

6. Lay the bag out flat on your work surface with the right side facing up. Place the lining fabric on top, right sides together, and pin at each end, raw edges aligning (note: the lining will be slightly larger at this point). Sew together at both ends with a 6mm (¼in) seam allowance (Fig. 2).

7. Refold the bag so that the seams that join the denim and the lining are on top of each other (see Fig. 3), and pin along these seams well. Now stitch along each side leaving a 7.5cm (3in) turning gap in one side of the lining.

8. Snip off the corners and turn the right way out. Stitch the opening closed, then tuck the lining into the denim. The red dot fabric should overlap the denim fabric by approx 1.3cm (½in). Press well.

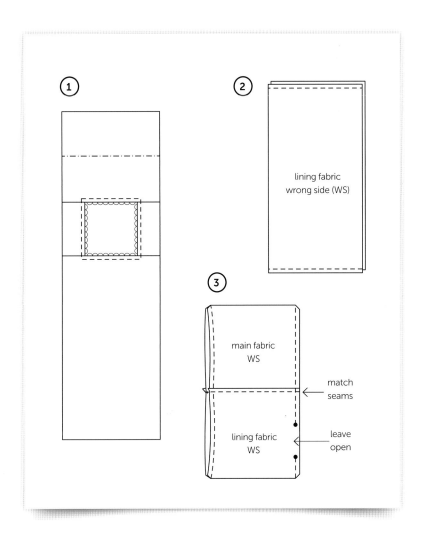

9. To make the bag flap, fold over the top of the bag by 10cm (4in) and press again. To keep the flap edges closed, sew the small popper (press stud) on the lining close to the bound edge.

10. Making sure that the flap is folded over, sew your bag handle to the back of the bag approx 1.3cm (½in) down from the top edge.

TIP

To make your own handle, cut a strip of leather 2.5 x 35cm (1 x 14in) long and use a hole punch or an awl to punch four small holes at each end to attach it to the bag.

ABC

EXTRA PROJECT:

Alphabet Hanging

I believe that all embroidery books need to include an alphabet so you can personalize your work but why stick them at the back of the book? They deserve some glory of their own, so I have used mine to create a sampler alphabet hanging – simple and easy. The redwork alphabet is framed with a selection of embroidered redwork borders, which are a great way to practise some of your stitches. I chose to bind the finished hanging like a little quilt but you could frame it with a junkyard frame.

Alphabet Hanging

YOU WILL NEED

34 x 37cm (13^1/$_2$ x 14^1/$_2$in) white cotton main fabric

50 x 55cm (20 x 21in) red check backing fabric

23cm (9in) of 107cm (42in) wide denim fabric for borders

Two skeins of DMC 321 coton à broder no. 16

50 x 55cm (20 x 21in) wadding (batting)

208cm (82in) 18mm (1^1/$_{16}$in) wide ready-made checked bias binding

FINISHED SIZE

48 x 73.5cm (19 x 29in)

STITCHES USED

Backstitch

Running stitch

Cross stitch

French knot

TO MAKE THE ALPHABET HANGING

1. From the denim fabric, cut two strips 34 x 9cm (13½ x 3½in) for the top and bottom borders and two strips 49.5 x 9cm (19½ x 3½in) for the side borders.

2. Transfer the border designs onto the white fabric panel. Start by drawing a box line 2.5cm (1in) from the edge of the fabric border. Then mark a box line 1.3cm (½in) inside the first marked line. You can then transfer three border designs of your choice (see Templates and Motifs), using these lines as a guide to help you to keep the design square. (See Transferring the Designs to select your preferred design transfer method.) First, mark the corner borders at the corners of your fabric and then tweak the designs so that they fit the length and width of the fabric. Mark a final box line approx 6mm (¼in) in from your third border design. Position the alphabet in the centre, placing it 2.5cm (1in) down from the top, which should leave a 4cm (1½in) gap at the bottom. This will be just perfect.

3. Pin, then sew the top and bottom black border strips to the shorter edges of the white cotton fabric, using a 6mm (¼in) seam. Then pin and sew the two longer denim border strips, again using a 6mm (¼in) seam. Press well.

4. Take your piece of wadding (batting) and lightly spray with spray adhesive following the manufacturer's instructions. Smooth the prepared front panel on top of the wadding (batting) and secure in place by stitching 6mm (¼in) all the way around the outside of the prepared cotton square.

5. Embroider the design using backstitch for the alphabet and most of the borders, with the following exceptions: work French knots at either side of the curvy line in the inner border and embroider the middle border by repeating three running stitches and a cross stitch.

6. Once your embroidery is complete, give your work a light press. Lightly spray the back of the wadding (batting) with spray adhesive and smooth the red check backing fabric onto it. (Alternatively tack (baste) the backing in place.) Working on the front, quilt in-the-ditch between the denim border and the embroidered cotton square, before binding with the ready-made checked bias binding (see Polar Bear Project: Cake Band for details of the mitred corners).

Design Your Own Motifs

It is so liberating when you are able to transfer your own thoughts and ideas into a piece of redwork and it really isn't that difficult. You can find inspiration for ideas in so many everyday household items including magazines, colouring books, packaging, vintage books, toys and photographs. The important thing is to keep your ideas simple, avoiding too many complicated lines.

You could, for example, use a photo of your house as the starting point for a design. Photocopy the photograph and then enlarge it. Use a black felt-tip pen to draw onto the photocopy just the main features of the house, without any fine details. Trace the drawing and tidy it up. Trace it again to get a neat copy; now you can add a few finer details if you wish. Make a final tracing, and your design is ready to transfer to your fabric, ready for embroidery. Alternatively, sketch a design from a favourite object, as I have for the train motif. I have included lots of my doodles in Templates and Motifs to inspire you and for you to use in projects of your own.

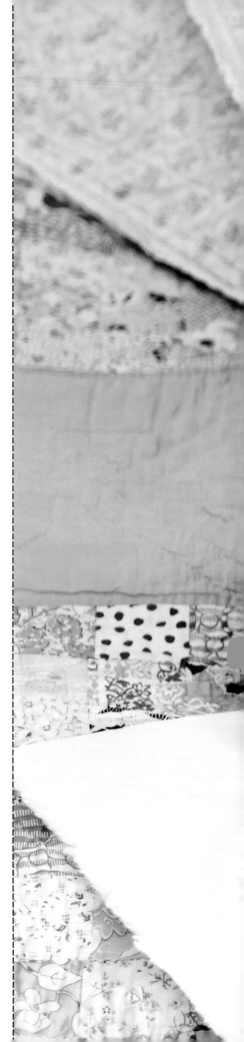

Design Your Own Motifs

I was inspired to make the sewing machine cushion from a 1950s children's sewing machine. First I took a photograph of the inspiration, enlarged the photo on a photocopier, drew around the outline, added a few details, traced a neater version, transferred it onto linen and stitched it. Voila!

The embroidery patch on the project bag was inspired by a front cover of a treasured book in my collection of vintage embroidery books. However, my little seamstress looks quite different, happily intent on her sewing task. This is an example of how you can adapt your inspiration to make a design your own.

Templates and Motifs

Note: the motifs and templates in this book are the actual size you will need to make the projects. They can be traced from the pages and used straight away. Alternatively, you can download a printable PDF of the templates and motifs from the following website: www.stitchcraftcreate.co.uk/patterns

It may be that you love a particular motif and would like to incorporate it into another project and therefore need to enlarge it or make it smaller. Go to your local photocopying shop (or most grocery stores have photocopiers) and get them to do this for you.

DAISY BROOCH

ALPHABET HANGING
Borders

ALPHABET HANGING
Alphabet

ABCDE
FGHIJK
LMNOP
QRSTU
VWXYZ

HEART

POLAR BEAR

SCISSORS

REDWORK QUILTS
Large Heart

REDWORK
HEARTS QUILT
Border Heart

KEY

HOUSE

DAISY

HAND

HOLLY

DOVE

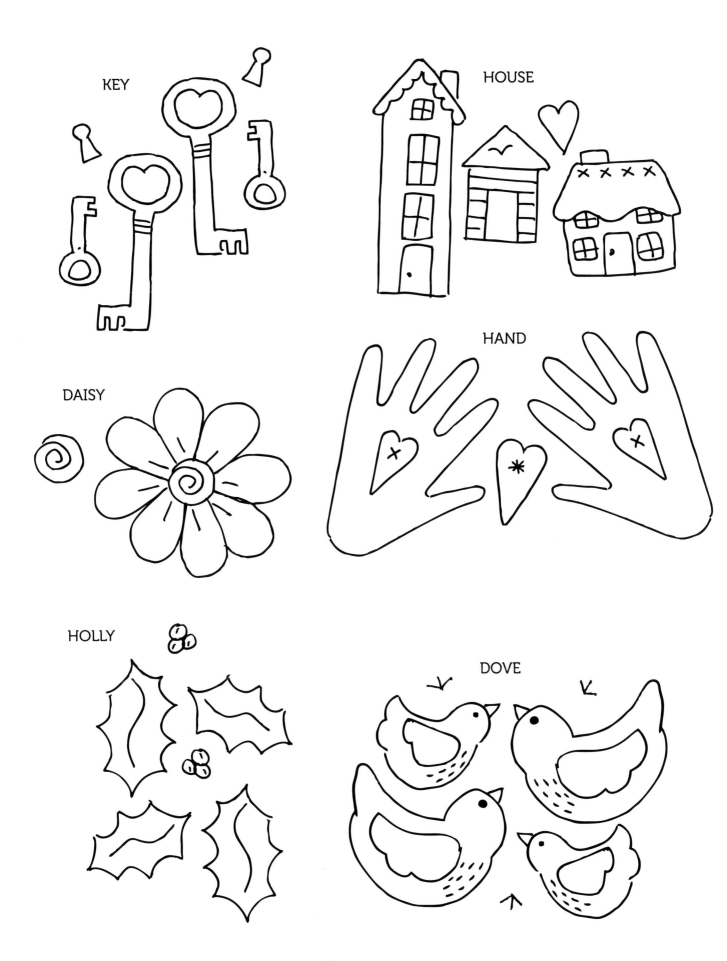

HEART CUSHION

PROJECT BAG

ADDITIONAL MOTIFS

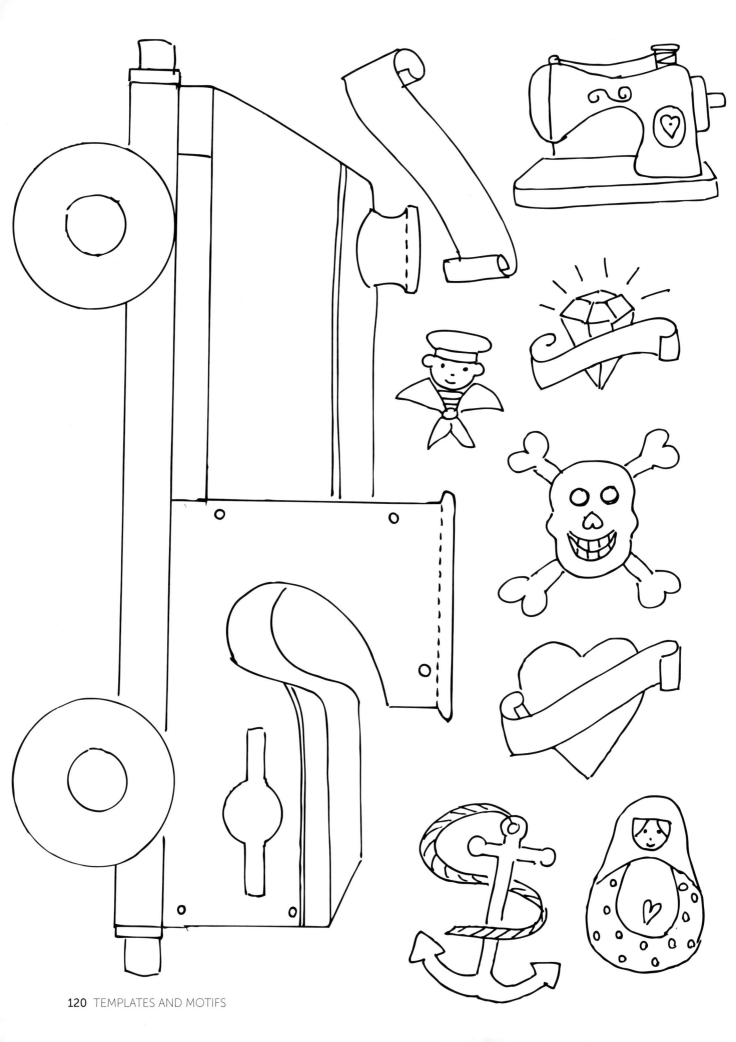

SCISSORS KEEPER
Note: seam allowances included

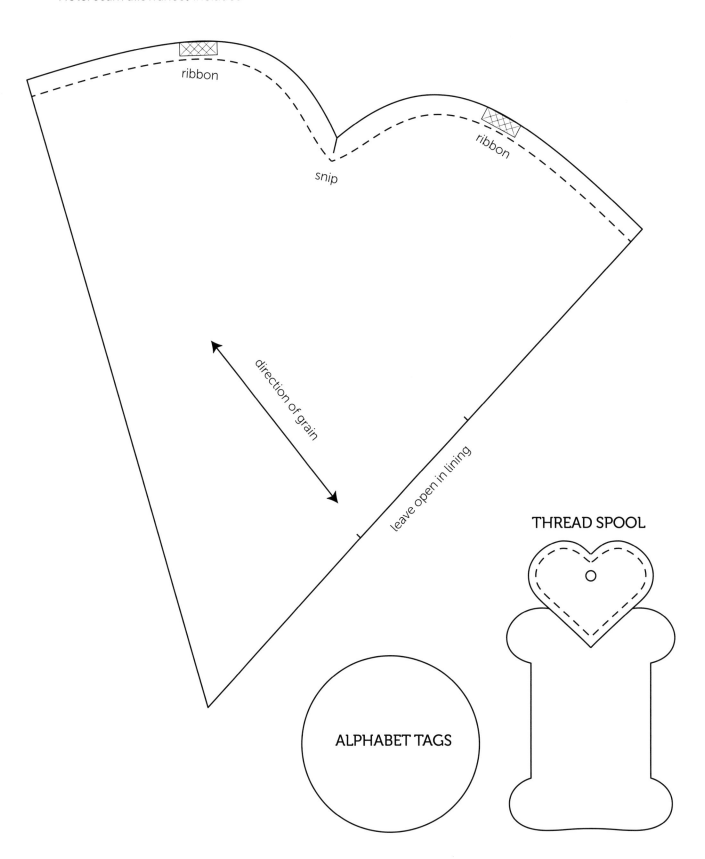

ribbon

ribbon

snip

direction of grain

leave open in lining

THREAD SPOOL

ALPHABET TAGS

WRIST SUPPORT
Note: seam allowances included

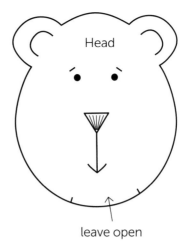

Head

leave open

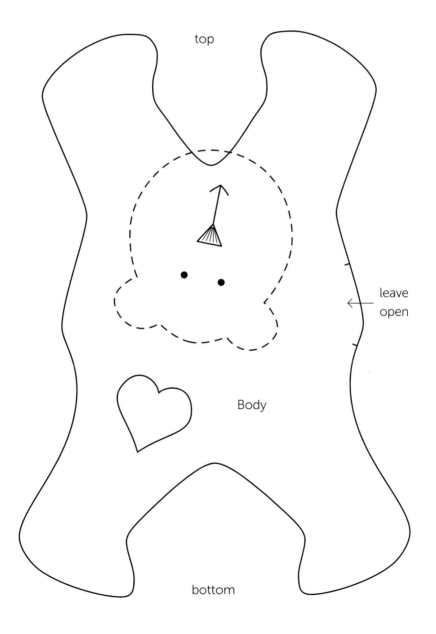

top

leave open

Body

bottom

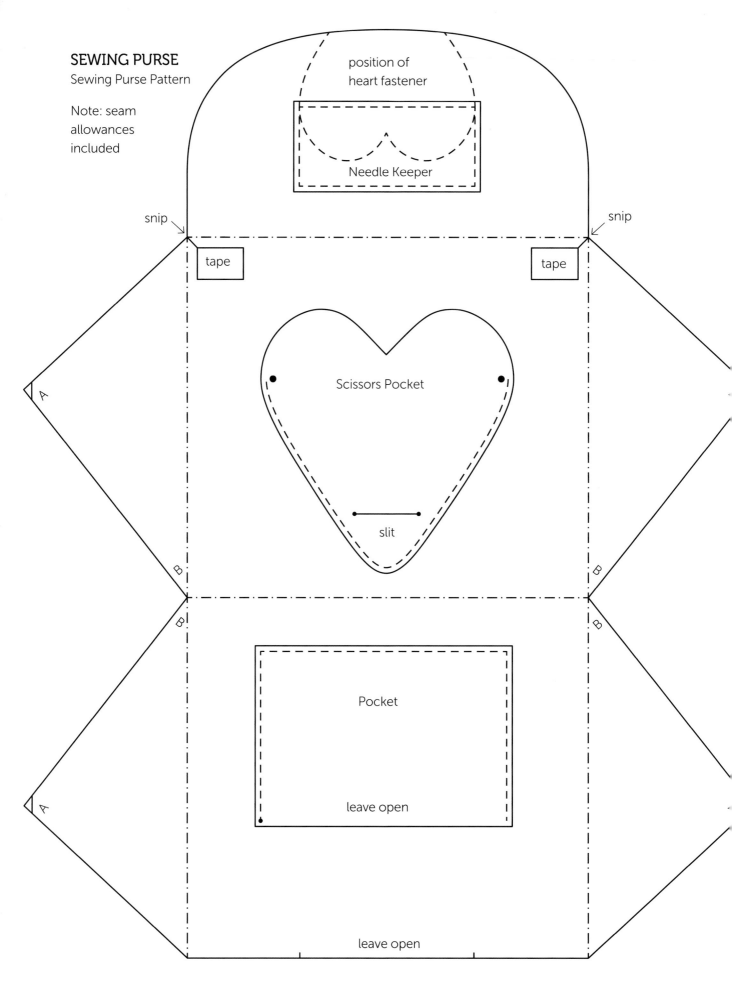

SEWING PURSE
Sewing Purse Pattern

Note: seam
allowances
included

position of
heart fastener

Needle Keeper

snip

snip

tape

tape

A

A

B

B

B

B

Scissors Pocket

slit

Pocket

leave open

A

A

leave open

SEWING PURSE
Heart Fastener

FLYING DOVE

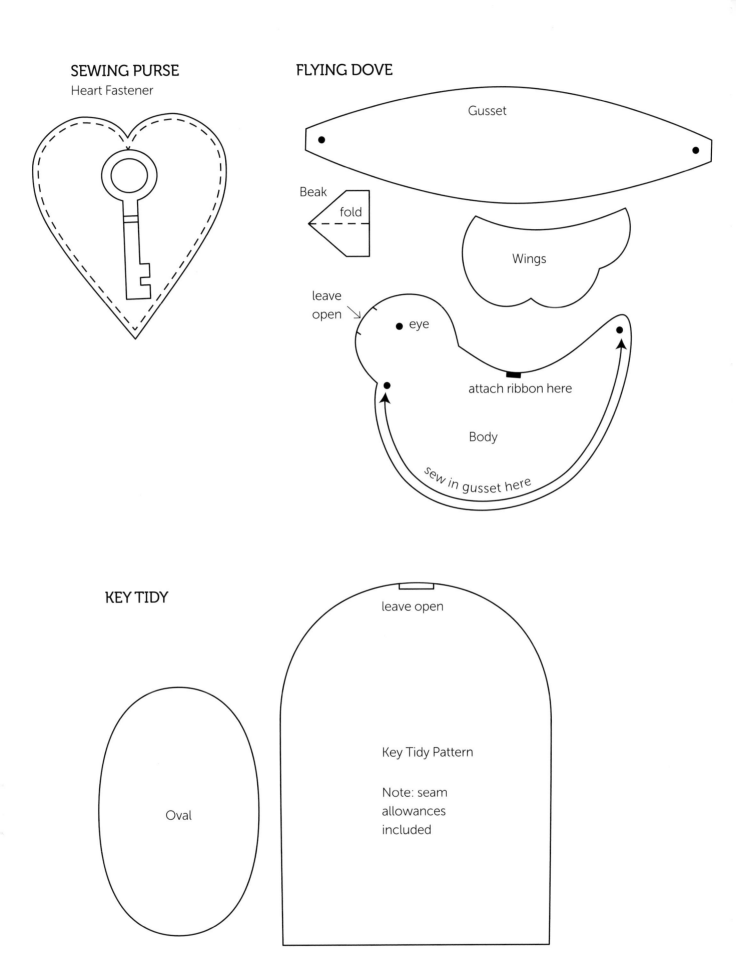

Gusset

Beak

fold

Wings

leave open

eye

attach ribbon here

Body

sew in gusset here

KEY TIDY

leave open

Oval

Key Tidy Pattern

Note: seam allowances included

Suppliers

DANDELION DESIGNS

Suppliers of threads, needles, linens and iron-on transfers for redwork projects, plus a huge selection of additional sewing patterns and haberdashery.

Website: www.dandeliondesigns.co.uk
Blog: www.dandeliondesigns.typepad.com
Email: mandy@dandeliondesigns.co.uk
Twitter: twitter.com/mandydandelion

UK SUPPLIES

BERNINA SEWING MACHINES
www.bernina.com

ANCHOR THREADS
www.coatscrafts.com

DMC THREADS
www.dmccreative.co.uk

STITCH CRAFT CREATE
www.stitchcraftcreate.co.uk

USA SUPPLIES

ANCHOR THREADS
www.coatsandclark.com

DMC THREADS
www.dmc-usa.com

FONS & PORTER
www.shopfonsandporter.com

MARTHA PULLEN
www.marthapullen.com

Acknowledgements

It's still a dream come true that I am given this opportunity to share my thoughts, ideas and projects with you in these beautifully produced books. The guys behind the scenes do a wonderful job and I consider myself very lucky to have editors Sarah Callard, Charlotte Andrew and Cheryl Brown to nurture me through the process, and to have students who encourage and inspire and help me – Iris Primrose yet again, and Linda too. But the people behind the scenes, who deal with my late nights, early mornings and erratic meal times, as well as living alongside the ridiculous amount of samples and patterns that I cannot bear to part with, are my very, very gorgeous family. Thank you. I love you all dearly. x

Index

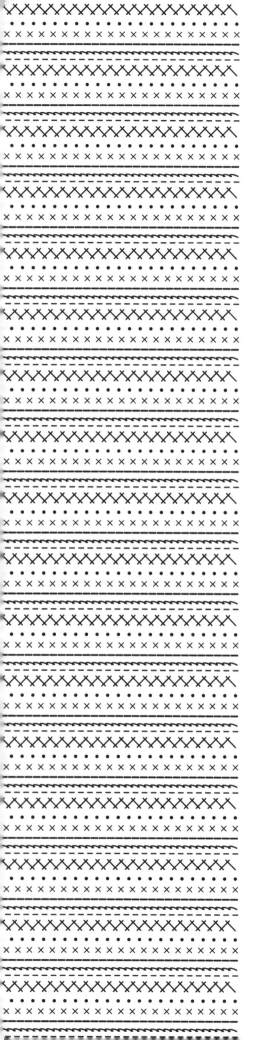

A DAVID & CHARLES BOOK
© F&W Media International, Ltd 2014

David & Charles is an imprint of F&W Media International, Ltd
Brunel House, Forde Close, Newton Abbot, TQ12 4PU, UK

F&W Media International, Ltd is a subsidiary of F+W Media, Inc
10151 Carver Road, Suite #200, Blue Ash, OH 45242, USA

Text and Designs © Mandy Shaw 2014
Layout and Photography © F&W Media International, Ltd 2014

First published in the UK and USA in 2014

Mandy Shaw has asserted her right to be identified as author of this work in
accordance with the Copyright, Designs and Patents Act, 1988.

A catalogue record for this book is available from the British Library.

ISBN-13: 978-1-4463-0502-7 paperback
ISBN-10: 1-4463-0502-3 paperback

Printed in Slovenia by GPS Group
F&W Media International, Ltd
Brunel House, Forde Close, Newton Abbot, TQ12 4PU, UK

10 9 8 7 6 5 4 3 2 1

Acquisitions Editor: Sarah Callard
Desk Editor: Charlotte Andrew
Project Editor: Cheryl Brown
Art Editor: Anna Fazakerley
Photographer: Sian Irvine
Senior Production Controller: Kelly Smith

F+W Media publishes high quality books on a wide range of subjects.
For more great book ideas visit: www.stitchcraftcreate.co.uk